MASQUERADE

THE LIFE GAME GOD PLAYS

- A GUIDE TO ENLIGHTENMENT -

◆

Daryl Chang

Front cover image: pixabay.com, Ruth Archer.
Rear cover image: pixabay.com, Briam Cute.

MASQUERADE: The Life Game God Plays, A Guide to Enlightenment
Daryl Chang
ISBN-13: 978-1-7389410-0-1

Personal Growth, Body Mind & Spirit, Self-help, Spirituality

I dedicate this book to my mom, my dad,
my siblings and my entire family.
God loves you. I love you. Now and forever.

I dedicate this book also to all who are searching and wanting
to live a true life of freedom, peace, love, joy, and happiness;
all who are willing to embrace the teachings to do so;
all who are determined, committed, and disciplined in
fulfilling the highest expression of the Divine Presence
within, their God-given purpose.

♦

To God who lives within you.
To the Overcomer you are.
Know who *you* are.

I thank you all, past and present, who have taken the time
to share your knowledge and wisdom; all who have crossed my path
and were my teachers; all who radiate their innate light to fill
darkness here; all who have shown courage and willingness
to seek, understand, and claim their divine inheritance.

I thank you, my friend, for taking the time to read this book.

I thank you God for entrusting me to write this book.
And for all the good things in my good life.

Herein lies an intriguing treatise on the lone identity revealed from the
many masks worn at the Greatest Masquerade Show on Earth.
This book you now hold in your hands will help you look in the mirror
with your spiritual eyes, and see the true self that gives
you the power to be conscious of your human self – *God*.
When you fully appreciate, accept, and know this truth,
it can be a profound moment in your spiritual development
to renew the personal life you live.

CONTENTS

♦

Preface

♦

There is a famous fable you might have heard of already. The story goes that if you put a frog into a pot of boiling water on a stovetop, it will jump out immediately because it knows otherwise that it will be cooked to its death. But if you put the frog in a pot of room temperature water, the frog will stay. If you turn the stove temperature up slowly, the frog will still not be inclined to jump out yet. The frog will obviously notice the heat but it acclimatizes to the gradual temperature change continually establishing a new normal for which it feels is tolerable. If the pot is left on the stovetop, the water will inevitably climb closer to a boiling point till the frog no longer finds it bearable to the point of life-threatening. How high do you think you can you raise the temperature such that the frog keeps enduring and entertaining its own demise? Well, that really depends on how conscious the frog is of what's going on, doesn't it?

You are the human being, the proverbial frog, immersed in a society and its environment, the proverbial pot of water, and the unGodly entity that is in a position of false illegitimate authority is the proverbial hand that controls the stove temperature. If the state of the existing world is becoming unbearable to you, does it not make sense for you to become more conscious of what is really going on, and to extricate yourself so that you continue to live life, preferably a joyous one?

I presuppose your answer is yes. Thus, I have written this book for you.

Prologue

◆

The prologue of a book is a window from the world of the reader to the inner life of the author. It is a way to answer two questions. Why did the author write this particular book? What will this book offer you as a reader?

This book I have written is a result of my lifelong search to understand this world I find myself in and why I am here. I have always had an intense desire to share with others. It brings me joy and appreciation when I do, and likewise when I see others do too. Sharing anything (ie. food, time, money, et cetera) is special, but knowledge particularly is one of the greatest gifts in this world because a person can receive it and enhance their life for a long time. In teaching and sharing things, some things become larger instead of smaller. And so I write this book in my own personal expression to help you understand a truth that many others, past and present, have also done in theirs.

This is a book for all people. It is a book for those lost in this world and seeking to find meaning in it; it is a book for those who do not actually know they are lost in this world and accept whatever reality is handed to them. Wisdom does not have to come when you are old; you can find it much sooner; and the sooner you gain it, the more this nonsensical world will make sense. Henceforth you can make forward progression instead of remaining in stagnation.

Though this book uses terms and phrases found in religion, it has no religious context and serves no religious purpose as you have come to perceive of any religion. Its aim is simply to point you to a truth which only you can determine, experience, and know for yourself. Many men have passed through our times and shared their teachings with people only to have people exalt them and not their intended teachings.

I cite the Four Reliances from the Tibetan Book of Living and Dying where it emphasizes more important than finding the teacher is finding and following the truth of the teaching. Rely on the message of the teacher not on his personality. Rely on the meaning not just the words.

Rely on the real meaning not on the provisional one. Rely on your wisdom mind not on your ordinary judgmental mind.

The title of this book, *MASQUERADE: The Life Game God Plays*, was chosen pensively. Oftentimes, fresh ideas are difficult to understand and accept. It helps when you can relate them to something more familiar. A masquerade ball is an occasion, event, or party in which those attending appear in costume wearing a mask. It is often turned into a game of "guess the guests" because the identities of participants are concealed by the masks they wear. Seeing life as a masquerade event can turn it into a humorous, whimsical, and enjoyable game rather than a painful, insufferable, and unpleasant one you've been possibly accustomed to for some time now.

This book has a simple premise. When each person knows and lives the truth of who they are, this unGodly nonsensical world will collapse. The Kingdom of God/Love/Heaven will be restored. You and I will be the better for it, as will mankind.

I trust you will have the courage, open-mindedness, humility, and willingness to enjoy, apply, and assimilate the information in this book. May this book help you to know the truth of God and yourself; in so doing, to be the love that you are and to fulfill the highest expression of the divine presence within yourself. In so doing, you enhance the manifestation of a good life (ie. health, abundance, love, joy, peace, happiness, et cetera) for yourself and inherently mankind. Through my own free will, so be it.

I wish you a good life. All the love, all the wisdom, and all the power to you.

Daryl Chang

Introduction

◆

There are some people, it seems, who vividly remember much of their childhood from the minuscule to the dramatic of details. I am not one of them. I am told that I was a very good child who was pleasurable and with a good temperament. I obeyed my parents. I was not mischievous or troublesome.

When I was a young child, I don't recall thinking too much. As I grew into a young adult though, I recognized that I thought a lot. I became more cognisant of things in this world. I began questioning things. In fact, I still do. I question everything. I question what people do that they think is "normal". I question why things are the way they are. I question always how things can be improved. I question many things.

This world where hatred, war and violence, people killing each other, intentional destruction of the planet, poverty, dis-ease, anger, fear, cruelty, greed, envy, et cetera existed was nonsensical to me. This world was unnatural to me. This world was unnatural for me. From an early age of being a so-called adult, I felt I did not belong here. I *really* did not want to be here. In fact, much of my adult life, I thought a lot about committing suicide. I'd say to myself, "Why do I think the things I do? Why do I have these thoughts? Where are these thoughts coming from? Do my friends or family have these thoughts? I don't think so. They don't seem to be or act like they do." Obviously, I didn't go through with it. You wouldn't be reading this book. I do recall several occasions where I was very close to acting on it but as it turned out, I didn't. Looking back, I had some angels – people in my life – nearby who must have sensed it because they wouldn't leave me alone. I think I would have done it otherwise. One day, I don't remember an exact time and date, but something happened without any warning. Suddenly, I noticed I no longer had suicidal thoughts. They just disappeared never to return again. With retrospect from the grace of time, I can now say with much gratitude that I am glad to be here still.

As mentioned, when I was no longer an innocent and naïve child and more self-conscious, everything in this world did not make sense to me.

I knew something wasn't right but I just couldn't put my finger on it. One day however without much fanfare, I gained clarity. Suddenly, this world made total sense to me. This world made no sense to me before because it was upside-down. Now, this world makes total sense to me because it *is* completely upside-down. It is *Heaven* upside-down – *Hell!* Does that make sense? It was a significant moment for me personally.

This world is upside-down. Everything is backward. Those false illegitimate unGodly authorities who are controlling the stovetop have been cleverly making subtle changes to society and its environment so that you wouldn't notice. Through deceit, you ongoingly acclimatized a new normal because you tolerated it. Before, you were innocent till you were proven guilty. Now, you are guilty till you prove you are innocent. Before, you had to opt-in in order to explicitly give your consent to others. Now you have to opt-out to remove consent from others to whom you never really gave; they just conveniently gave themselves consent first to justify the opt-out action required. Before, you were healthy until nature proved that you were sick. Now, you are automatically considered sick until you take their fraudulent tests to inanely prove you are not. Before, you were sovereign with the birthright of freedom until you broke a law created by a false illegitimate authority. Now, you have increasingly restricted freedom (ie. a slave) until you unnecessarily protest for freedom so that the same false illegitimate authority may reward you with some semblance of sovereignty that was originally yours.

Whatever is not yet upside-down is being tactfully flipped so that it does not cause an immediate uproar from those unconscious. This way, there is minimal disruption to the process. The proverbial hand that controls the stovetop temperature has made you normalize the unGodly things in this world: death, destruction, war, violence, hatred, anger, fear, worry, envy, greed, competition, poverty, dis-ease, et cetera. You have tolerated the intolerable and accepted the unacceptable. You believe you have no power to end it but you are mistaken. You have always had the power of your own accord to jump out of their pot but you have chosen not to. When the temperature of restricted freedom becomes overly critical, you the proverbial frog still unconscious, may not be in a condition to jump out of the proverbial pot on which the controller has already begun securing a lid. You have been an active participant in the partaking of your own death.

Daryl Chang

When I finally gained clarity, I knew definitively that this world was not my original home. I no longer succumbed to it nor accommodated it. All I had to do was figure out how to turn the world right-side up. This was the apparent enigma. I was confident though that I would succeed because it had been achieved by a few. If one can do it, then all can. If I can do it, then you can too.

CHAPTER 1
A Word on Words
♦

Before you and I get going, I'd like to say a few words on words.

Words are one of many human forms that are created and exist for communication and expression. From an intellectual standpoint, they are deemed important and necessary to identify and describe the things in this world we live in. In reality, each and every thing in the world exists in spite of the words we use to do as such. Words are but symbols of symbols. The sun shines even without being called the sun, a tree grows even without being called a tree, and water nourishes even without being called water.

Words by its own nature ironically pose a hazard in its very purpose of communication and expression. Words require the understanding of other words to understand the meaning of the word itself. We assume that the dictionary meaning applied to a word, however it resulted, is a "true" expression of its intellectual meaning. Your thoughts, actions, and beliefs will be influenced by your interpretation of the word's meaning. If the meaning or premise is not "true", then how you operate may in turn be false.

Despite a dictionary meaning, every word is subject to an individual's unique understanding and interpretation of it. Conflict between people results because there is no synchronicity amongst persons in the understanding and interpretation of the meaning behind a word.

Words ultimately create separation. As soon as something is named or labelled, it creates separation. The naming of a "Being" automatically puts one object "here" and the other object "there". It inherently separates two objects (eg. You and I, You/I and God, Christian and Non-Christian, Canadian and American, Black and White, Humans and Animals). Though the word is necessary to discern things, it unintentionally obscures the connectedness between them, the oneness of all. Without a diligent conscious recognition of this, the Truth gets lost to the point where it eventually does not exist.

Words belong to the world of form; they cannot truly express that which has no form. Admittedly, no matter how much someone tells us about something or describes something, we will never actually know until we try and experience it for ourselves. Words may be used to describe or express the meaning of an object or idea, but it will never be adequate or complete. A person must see and experience the object to fully understand and appreciate the object itself. For instance, an apple may be described as sweet, crunchy, and juicy but the words alone are insufficient for a person to fully understand what an apple is if he's never had one. A person must experience what we have labelled an apple to fully know for themself what it is.

The moment you try to describe or explain anything, you have actually lost its meaning. Therein lies the challenge and irony of our intellectual world.

Recognize that all words exist because its origin is from Oneness. This is particularly evident with words that express dualities or polarities (ie. deemed opposites); they are on the same continuum. The key to everything in life is a complete understanding and appreciation of Oneness: *God*.

No matter what your belief is, undeniably, there is a "source" of creation. This "source" has been given many names such as God, Source, Creator, Divine, the Power, Higher Intelligence, Creative Principle, and Universal Consciousness. Whichever word you are comfortable with, it is simply the attempt to label that creative "source" of existence which goes beyond our human intellectual comprehension. I use the word *God* as the Source of creation because it is short and sweet, and I am comfortable with it.

Throughout the book, I often use the pronoun "you". It is used as an impersonal term for expressive purposes only. You will see that I use words like unGod, unGodly, unChrist, and dark. I intentionally do not use negative prefixes or common labels, names, or titles that have come to denote the opposite or against life. God is all-encompassing so He can have no opposite. The imposed duality is an illusion. Such particular words create illusions of separation and I'd like to discontinue this proliferation. I avoid them also because I can feel the negative energy stemming from them, especially when I say them verbally out loud.

Words are of great consequence because they are powerful and are weapons, wielded in love or fear. The usage of words like bad and evil in this unGodly world have persistently reinforced them as opposites to good. Good versus evil has no real existence but are relative terms descriptive of outside conditions looked at from different viewpoints. The principle of Oneness is masked.

I typically do not use these words so as not to propagate this illusion. That or those which are "bad or evil", I identify them as ignorant, meaning of low consciousness. This is more suitable because it does not normally imply an opposite but a state. Though I do not use the word ignorant with a demeaning and condescending intention, I generally avoid using it in the book because I know that it has that connotation attached to it. When you see me use the traditional words "bad or evil", it is for illustrative purposes to suit the context.

When I say un –this or un –that, I do not mean it is the opposite of this or that. I mean "that which is not wholly that"; or "that which is less than that". So, unGod is that which is not wholly God or that which is less than God. Further, dark is lesser light; evil is lesser good. It is akin to a dimmer switch. A dimmer switch is not an on/off switch that delineates an illusion of duality of light and dark; of good and evil. It varies the one quality to more or less.

I will also use terms such as Universal Mind, One Mind, Universal Consciousness, One, Oneness, Superconscious, and Father. God is all in all so these are God by another name. They are synonymous and interchangeable for all intents and purposes. Why the different usage then? I just feel that the word used sounds more appropriate within the context. That's all.

CHAPTER 2
The Contemplation, Revelation, and Exhilaration

♦

I am a thinker. I have always asked questions. How did I get here? Where did I come from? Why am I here? What is my purpose? What am I supposed to be doing here? Where do my thoughts come from? Why do I desire the things I want? Where do my desires come from? Why do I not consistently experience the things I know I want? Why do I long for things like peace, joy, and happiness yet they seem so elusive? Why is the world in the current state it finds itself in? Why does man seem to like destroying his own kind and the planet he lives on? Why does it seem that most people not think or care about the answers to these questions? Have you asked yourself such questions too?

I don't just ask simple questions like the abovementioned. I ask provocative ones too. What time does the squirrel in my backyard get up in the morning? Does it have to go to a squirrel school in order to learn how to survive and live life? When it inadvertently hurts its paw, does it seek out a squirrel doctor to help heal it? Does it constantly worry about how to make money in order to provide for itself and survive? Does it get up every morning to go to work so as to "make a living"? Does it need permission from some squirrel authority to walk along any property or part of God's kingdom? Are there are any creatures in this world that do any of the things man does?

Does the tulip look at the rose, feel envious, and wish that it was a rose? Does the tulip rise each day and ponder what it is to do today, what it should have done yesterday, and what it should do tomorrow? Does the tulip judge itself whether it is beautiful or not? Does the tulip care about the opinion of others and ask the rose whether it is pretty or not?

Does the sun look down on a thief and decide to not shine on him because it judges him as bad? Does the sun ask anything of the flower that it shines on? Does the sun become sad if no one worships it?

Why do gas stations install a huge sign to post their prices and then plant a tree beside it to block its view? If a smoker flicks his cigarette butt littering outside, why doesn't he do the same inside his home instead of using an ashtray? If a tree sits outside all day in the sun and grows enormously, why do people think the sun is "bad" and cause that dis-ease? Yes, there are infinite questions that flow into my mind constantly but I digress.

This world I seem to live in is not home to me. Somewhere in my mind, I know this is true. What I know I cannot explain but I feel it. I have felt it my entire life that there's something wrong with this world. I feel an outsider here. It is a persistent feeling that is like an eternal candle flickering inside me.

In much of the past, I thought a lot about things. I wondered about many things. I pondered over many things. While I admittedly did much thinking, I realize now that I didn't really contemplate things. But one day, I contemplated. I contemplated life. Not life as in my life but life of all things. That is, the existence of existence.

I contemplated on a seed. I put a seed into the soil. Then in a relatively short time, it sprouts, breaks the surface, and grows. I asked, "How does it do this? Did it go to plant school during the time it was underground to earn a degree to learn how to do this? Really, how does it know how to do this?" Then I thought, "There must be a higher power, a higher intelligence that's doing this."

I then contemplated on a bird flying in the sky. I asked, "How does it do this? Does it go to some bird aviation school to earn a degree to learn how to do this? Really, how does it know how to do this?" Then I thought about the birds that fly south every winter always finding their way to the same place. I asked the same question, "How do they do this?" The same thought came to mind, "There must be a higher power, a higher intelligence that's doing this."

I contemplated many other things in nature asking the same question. I got the same answer.

Next, I contemplated on a mother having a baby. At no time does the mother provide instructions to the things inside her body to do this and do that to grow the baby. The baby just develops. Just like the seed, I asked, "How does it do this?" There is a higher power, a higher intelligence that's doing this.

I finally turned on myself. I contemplated on my breathing. Do I "do" breathing? That is, do I instruct myself, my body, on how to go about breathing? No I don't. It just happens. Do I "do" circulating blood? Do I instruct my body on how to circulate my blood and distribute the oxygen throughout? No I don't. It just happens. Do I "do" digesting food? Do I instruct my body and coordinate all my organs to digest my food? No I don't. It just happens. So if I'm not doing the breathing, the blood circulating, and the food digesting, then who's doing it? I'll give you a clue. It's not Peter, Paul, or Mary. Did you answer the question yourself? It's the higher power, the higher intelligence. It's God. God is in me, just as He is in the seed, the flower, the tree, the bird, the squirrel, the sun, the moon, and so on and so on. He is in everything.

God who is in me is also in you. He is the lone identity behind the illusion of a unique mask worn by every fellow human being. This is the Ark of the Covenant, the silent acceptance of the secret relationship between God the Creator and me, the created. This truth is true for every person on this physical Earth.

I will tell you now that this discovery, though extraordinary when it struck me, isn't actually anything new per se. This is what Jesus was teaching all along. Prior to this moment, the scriptures were still a bit cryptic to me. At long last, I altogether grasped it. Jesus was the first person to contemplate himself and figure it out. He was the Pioneer, the Way-shower, the Master Metaphysician. He tried to convey God the Creative Principle and our relation to this Creative Principle. He was crucified by men of limited thinking, unconscious of who they were, for blasphemy; it is *still* going on today. He demonstrated it. He proved it. He did all the work. He revealed it as an established fact. My work now is to simply accept it, begin where He left off, and proceed toward my full expression.

This brings to mind Confucius who stated, "By three methods we may learn wisdom. First, by reflection, which is noblest; second, by experience, which is bitterest; and third, by imitation, which is easiest."

The discovery of this truth gives you a fresh perspective. With the discovery of this truth, you begin to perceive a new reality. With the discovery of this truth, you begin to see God in all things: the sun, the moon, the birds, the flowers, the trees, the rocks, the earth, the mountains, the animals, et cetera. With the discovery of this truth, you begin to see God behind the mask and costume that every human being wears: the good person, the bad person, the ugly person, the beautiful person, the cripple, the vagrant, the drug addict, the tyrant, et cetera. With the discovery of this truth, you begin to see the divine soul, the seed or child of God learning and developing himself to hopefully become who he ultimately is (in his own unique expression): *God*.

The aforementioned is quite a revelation. This is a very profound moment. Oftentimes, something simple yet unfathomable is not so easy to accept as true. But this is just a habit from your limited thinking because you are not conscious of who you are yet. This is the irony of your current predicament. I'll take a pause here so you can let what you've just read to truly sink in. Reread it if you'd like. I'll wait for you.

Okay, how great is this? When I finally realized this truth, when I truly understood it, when I fully appreciated it, and when I wholly accepted it, a weight lifted off my shoulders and I felt light. I smiled. Then I laughed. Then I felt joy. Then I felt peace. Then I felt silly. I felt silly because I thought, "All this time, I've been trying to figure things out on my own, trying to figure what to do, and how to achieve this and attain that. I've been expending time, effort, and energy when I didn't have to. God was within me all this time. And if I was like the seed and simply allowed Him to do what He does, then all things would be taken care of. All good things would come to me because that's what He does." Then after a moment of exhilaration, I said, "Wow. Well okay then. Let's get to work."

CHAPTER 3
God and His Kingdom
♦

So now I know that God is within me. I am one with God. Before I proceed, I have to be clear on what this means. I have to be clear on who *He* is. How do I define or describe God?

God is the formless invisible animating intelligent force of energy that penetrates, permeates, and fills the spaces and interspaces of the universe of which it is itself. God is also all the visible forms produced from its formless invisible Self. God is the sum of all things visible and invisible.

First and foremost, to put it succinctly, God is love. Any and all words used to describe Him stems from this and are essentially synonymous. God is intelligence, consciousness, life, perfection, purity, power, eternity, infinity, lightness, unlimitedness, substance, joy, peace, harmony, happiness, compassion, kindness, gratitude, abundance, oneness, wholeness, connectedness, calmness, stillness, inclusion, expansion, freedom, non-judgment, non-attachment, non-resistance, health, youth, beauty, clarity, knowledge, and wisdom. God is everything. God is all things good only.

In brief, God is omnipotent, omniscient, and omnipresent. That is, He is all-powerful, all-knowing, and all-around. God is all in all.

God is eternal and infinite. This means that He has no beginning and no ending; He is the *circle of existence*. He is perpetually expanding.

If God did not expand, then that would mean He was not eternal and infinite. But He *is* eternal and infinite. He must continuously expand for that is His nature. It is unnatural for Him to not expand Himself. God must exhibit who He is always, inherent by His eternal and infinite nature.

Because of His eternal and infinite nature, He cannot be contained. God is the water flowing through the tunnel with extraordinary energy. His pressure and force is immense. If you try to suppress or contain Him however you do, He will blow the lid off. Any attempts to restrict His expansion will fail.

God is perfect good. God is wholly love, joy, peace, and all things good. God is persistent in maintaining His perfect good state. If God strays from the perfect good state, even slightly, He will always automatically correct Himself to reinstate His perfect good condition.

Now that I know who God is, I subsequently know the kingdom of God – *God Consciousness*. As God is within, the kingdom of God is within. I call the kingdom of God affectionately "God Country". In God Country, there exists only love and all its relatives; all things pure and good. There is complete peace and harmony. There is rich abundance of all good things for everyone and whose store is inexhaustible; anything needed or wanted is always available. There is constant gratitude. There is no separation or division of any kind: borders, countries, religions, and castes do not exist. Everything is choreographed with elegant precision and unfaltering intelligence.

All are selfless and cooperate for the highest good and serve mankind. All of nature is treated with respect and care. Money has no relevance and does not exist. Soul fulfillment and satisfaction is the driving force behind all that you do. You are as the flower. You enter the world with a unique perspective and talents, which enable you to blossom an aspect of natural intelligence that has never been expressed before. You freely express your beauty without reservation because there are no restraints for survival.

All are equal. There is no one, seen or unseen, who can ever be greater than you, and there is no one who can ever be less than you. All know they are one.

This is my home. I know it.

There is no one above you except the Creator, *God*. There should never be anyone between you and the Creator, *God*. God is the sole authority. Anyone between you and the Creator – *God* – is a false illegitimate authority acting dishonourably under a false claim.

God Country was the original Earth. The spiritual decay of mankind has been in constant deterioration for quite some time now resulting in the current Earth we find ourselves living in. You can help restore God Country by walking the spiritual path with God and not the path of the UnGod.

God is all in all. I am one with God. You are one with God. You are an individual part of the Universal Mind, the One Mind. You *are* One Mind. When you truly understand, accept, and know this truth, you cannot and will not say, "… but I am just one person. I'd like to but I can't change the world. What's the difference?" You cannot just know the truth, you must also live it. By knowing and living the truth of who you are, that is *God*, you restore the One Mind. Hence, you restore God Country. Walk the path.

CHAPTER 4
The True Self

♦

So now I know that God is within me and I know who God is. It is clear now that I am not entirely who I thought I was before. I am cognisant now that there are actually two beings within me. I need to be clear on what this means. I need to be able to readily discern the two. I need to be clear on who I am wholly. Who am I really then when I use the word "I"?

To distinguish the two beings, for clarity sake, I label one "Big-I" and the other "Lil-i". *I* and *i* are two unique forms but represent the same character.

Big-I is God, the True (Higher) Self, the Christ, the Master, the Divine Being, the Divine Mind, the Higher Consciousness, the Creator, the Unlimited. The Big-I knows He is One with all. The Big-I is concerned mostly about being. The Big-I is wise.

Lil-i is the unGod or ego, the False Self, the unChrist, the Servant, the human being (personality), the human mind, the lower consciousness, the Competitor, the limited. The Lil-i thinks he is separate from One and all. The Lil-i is concerned mostly about doing. The Lil-i is clever.

Lil-i is my ego and I affectionately call it doG. I find it fitting to call the ego the "dog" – with a capital G – in me because it is God spelled backwards, and a dog is supposed to be a loyal companion who obeys its Master. As you know, a dog needs to be trained; otherwise it becomes the master, and the Master the servant. I've given my doG the name *daryl* with a lowercase d, not to confuse it with my Earthly-given name *Daryl* representing the whole of me.

When I use the word "I" and its relatives like me, my, and myself, I do so meaning the whole of me: my soul, the inner child. I am a child of God, a seed of His Greatness. I am an Observer of both my human self and Divine Self. If I need to make a clear distinction, I will emphasize between the use of Big-I or Lil-i. At my discretion, I may use instead the labels God or doG.

So Big-I and Lil-i share the same temple, my body. When I am conscious of myself, both are in their rightful place and in synchronization; they serve each other well and live in harmony. When I am not conscious of myself, I allow Armageddon, a battle to ensue between God and unGod, Christ and unChrist, Master and Servant, Big-I and Lil-i; disharmony results.

If there is a conflict within me, it indicates that God does not have full control, meaning that doG is overreaching its position or role. If doG is involved in any of my behaviour or actions, then I will stray from God Country. This means I will have experiences to some degree that are unGodly such as fear, anger, ill-health, lesser of abundance, love, joy, and peace. I will struggle through or have to deal with undesirable negative conditions.

God is within me. God flows and works through me. God, the Big-I, is the Power who gives *me* the power to be conscious of myself, the human being.

Now that I've discerned the two beings conceptually, I need to discern them practically. I need to be clear and certain always who is speaking to me when I hear an inner voice. When I am able to do this, then I'll be able to know if and when to obey what is said to me.

For the most part, it's quite easy to discern when God is speaking to me and when God is not speaking to me but rather the doG is. This is because I know who God is.

How do I tell whose voice is speaking (ie. God or doG)?
- If the voice is encouraging and motivating me for personal growth, it's God.
- If the voice is directing me toward spiritual pleasure and growth (ie. joy, peace, happiness, et cetera), it's God.
- If the voice desires something but isn't attached to it, it's God.

- If the voice is driven by physical desire, pleasure, or sensation, it's not God. It's doG.
- If the voice is driven by selfish motive for selfish gain, it's not God. It's doG.
- If the voice is negative feeling (ie. shame, guilt, fear, et cetera), it's not God. It's doG.
- If the voice is critical or judgmental, it's not God. It's doG.
- If the voice has ill-intent, then it's not God. It's doG.
- If the voice is persuading me to be lazy and remain comfortable in undesirable conditions, then it's not God. It's doG.
- If the voice desires something, particularly an object, and is really attached to it, then it's not God. It's doG.
- If the voice is trying to figure out how to do something, it's not God. It's doG.
- If the voice is rushing me, then it's not God. It's doG.

It helps to consciously listen to the conversation you have with yourself, reflect on what is said, and determine who is speaking to you. When you do this regularly, you'll get better at identifying if it's Big-I or Lil-i. It's like eavesdropping on the conversation of the couple sitting beside you at the café. You'll be able to sense the characters of the two in a short time.

Here are two examples of internal dialogues. See if you can identify if it's Big-I or Lil-i speaking.

"I'm truly blessed. I have a beautiful home, a great family, and a good life. I have everything I need. I think I will write a book to help others struggling to understand how they can overcome their troubles. I send love to all those politicians who obviously have no clue about their own egos and don't realize they don't need to be so greedy."

"I know it's not good for my health right now but I think I'll have a beer. It's only one drink. It's not going to kill me. The neighbour will probably be impressed when I get that Ferrari. I wish the PM would drop dead, he's such a $#@%& tyrant!"

Were you able to tell who's who?

Big-I was speaking in the former. He showed gratitude. He thought about a way He could serve others. And He was able to show love to those He recognized aren't really conscious of what they're doing.

Lil-i was speaking in the latter. He persuaded me to give into my physical pleasure. He was concerned about what the neighbour thought. And he was hoping for another's misfortune.

It's possible you're unfamiliar as yet and have trouble detecting who is speaking to you. An alternative means to do this somewhat is to work backwards. All is spiritual. The physical is spiritual manifest. As such, the external physical is always giving you feedback on what's going on inside spiritually. It's always confirming to you whether God or doG is in control for the most part. You can tell who the Master of you is; who holds the power within you; who is speaking to you the majority of the time. For instance, if your home is messy, if you're struggling with poverty, and if you hoard stuff, then these are indications that your doG is speaking most of the time. This is vital for you to understand and know because the feedback informs you to return to your true self and make adjustments to your thoughts.

There is another means that helps me determine who is speaking. I find it helps to remember the master-servant relationships of the parts within me. God is the Master of my soul, my soul is the master of my mind, and my mind is the master of my body. I surrender my body to be ruled by mind. I surrender my mind to be governed by my soul. And I surrender my soul to the guidance of God. That is, I work top down: *God-soul-mind-body*. If it seems I'm being ruled from the bottom up, I know I'm going astray.

This is to say for example. If I give into a physical pleasure though my mind objects, then my body is the master and my mind is the servant. My mind should be the master. If I give into my mind to be lazy though my soul says I want to grow spiritually, then my mind is the master and my soul is the servant. My soul should be the master. If I give into my emotions, then my emotions are my master, not my mind. I must be in control of my own mind. When I remind myself of the hierarchy – *God-soul-mind-body*, I discern who is acting as my master. I can better ascertain if my True Self is directing me.

CHAPTER 5
The False Self

◆

The ego is the false self. It is your human personality. It is the unGod and the unChrist, who lives in the same residence as God and Christ. The irony is, it is a part of you and it is not a part of you. It allows you to discern what is not you so that you can know what is you. You cannot have, appreciate, and know joy without having, appreciating, and knowing sorrow. Once you know both, then you know One, and then you know to know only One: *God*.

The ego is a part of you like your hand is. It is a tool you use for your human experience. It is an unseen part of your mind that is your assistant, your nanny, your custodian, your protector, your cheerleader, and your motivational speaker of the inner child. If you understand its nature and function, and know how to use it, it serves you well. It is akin to understanding that a hammer is for installing nails not screws, and then knowing how to pound it properly for efficient nailing.

The unchecked ego is very clever. He knows he is not the true master. He knows he has no real power. But he knows that possibly, *you* don't know this either. So he keeps quiet about this fact and doesn't overtly admit this. In lieu of your ignorance, he lets you think that he is the master. He creates the illusion that he has power. He lets you think that he is you and you are him. By you remaining silent and not proclaiming that you do not consent to his rule, he conveniently and arrogantly takes this as implied consent of his authority. You have handed him keys to his own fabricated kingdom.

When I use the term "unchecked ego", I mean that it is an ego, whose doG's leash has been loosened. When the leash is loosened, you are allowing the doG to more freely run around a bit. If you are not diligent, the doG may break its leash and run rampant, thus allowing it (Lil-i) to become your false master. Once it breaks the leash, it may be difficult to corral. In fact, the doG will lead you to all kinds of paths you didn't care for. Picture someone walking his dog and you will understand what I mean. The doG loves to roam and explore.

A checked ego then is one who is in its rightful place as the servant to the Master within you, the soul.

Everyone has an ego and most, if you observe, unconsciously give their doG some free rein. The true Master is God (Big-I). When you are conscious of whom the Master is, you will keep a tight leash on your doG always. When you are unconscious and give some free rein, it means you allow the doG to freely act somewhat of its own accord and desired direction. This means you are voluntarily giving him some control, impacting how you walk, as opposed to you being in unremitting full control.

Even if you think you are a "good" person, you can tell immediately if your ego is unchecked to some degree because your actions and behaviour will be unGodly. "I am a good person," I can hear you say. For example, if you get angry for whatever "good" reason and let it take over you for even a second, your ego is still unchecked. Anger is not a loving attribute and The Big-I, your true Master, is always loving. I am not saying you will not or should not get angry, but when you are conscious, the Big-I with a checked ego will catch the emotion, and mitigate it immediately.

When people use the sole term ego, they are referring to an unchecked ego. This ego can be problematic. I qualify this because a checked ego can be beneficial to you when you encounter an unchecked ego. A checked ego, whose Master is the Big-I, will not be intimidated by an unchecked ego because you now know who holds true power. Your doG, loyal servant to you, will protect you from another doG. Even though your neighbour's doG barks loud and growls at you trying to harm and impose their will on you, your fearless doG will stand its ground. As mentioned, your doG is a loyal companion who is a valuable resource to you when you need it.

When I use the sole term ego (for economic sake) henceforth, I imply the unchecked ego.

The ego incites you to act out of negativity. Its actions are based and governed by fear. It has a lust for attachment to things. It feeds off your thoughts and emotions; and off your past and future. It is selfish and vain.

The ego is obsessed with having an identity of its own. This makes sense because he is not God. He thinks he is separate from God. So he identifies with an object, a role, an idea, anything that is external. For example, he identifies with having many things that make him feel important: the car, the title, the brand name clothes he wears, et cetera; with the role of a mother, a wife, a daughter, a nurse, et cetera; with the religion of a Catholic, Protestant, Muslim, et cetera. If you take away the identity he finds in these, he is lost. He doesn't know what to do with himself then.

The ego is incessantly judging, comparing, and competing. It is always concerned more about taking and getting, less about giving and serving others. It is concerned about what others think and having their approval. It prefers to fit in and so conforms to the majority, afraid of being singled out from what everyone is doing, even if what they're doing is immoral and wrong. In reality, he's like most bullies. He's actually weak, a coward who pretends to be strong and unafraid.

The ego can become obsessive about being the master of you. In essence, he loves power and control. Lil-i will use two strategies on you. He can be overly negative and make you feel inferior to undermine you. He can deflate your self-image. You'll have low self-esteem, self-confidence, and self-importance. This might transmute itself into extreme shyness, indecisiveness, and apprehension. You may have a hard time looking people in the eye, talking to them, or standing up to them.

Conversely, Lil-i can be overly positive and make you feel superior to bolster you. He can inflate your self-image. You'll have excessive self-esteem, self-confidence, and self-importance. This might transmute itself into extreme boldness, decisiveness, and belligerence. You may come across as overbearing, arrogant, and abrasive.

The ego doesn't care which way you go. Either way, he exerts power and control over you. The road you take is influenced by your environment. He will leverage whichever negative or positive tactics proves convenient.

The ego doesn't stop at you. Lil-i is compulsive in trying to extend his power beyond where he is situated. As such, when he encounters another ego, he asserts himself to gain more power and control. He is ambitious and insatiable.

It is easy to understand then that when two individual egos meet, there is a power struggle. An ego is either dominant or subservient. There can be two possible results. A subservient ego will succumb to a dominant one. If on the other hand, both egos are relatively dominant, an unrelenting conflict ensues. This conflict will typically display itself as mental, verbal, and physical abuse toward each other.

I trust you now see that if you do not control your ego, you can become easily manipulated and mired in your own chaotic world, as well as the chaotic world of others. It is a bottomless pit, the proverbial hell many perceive exist.

"How do I control my ego?" I can hear you ask.

I view it the way I would with a dog or a child. I want to establish myself as the Master/parent. I want to command respect. I want to be firm. I want to instil discipline. But I want to exhibit love still. I don't want to abuse it or be overly harsh because if I do, I'm abusing myself. You know this too. If I impudently yell at a child or dog, it may obey but more so in fear than from respect.

For instance, in speaking to my doG, I'd say, "*daryl*, be quiet," in a firm but calm voice. Because I just started training him, he'll test me. So again, I say, "*daryl*, be quiet!" still in a calm voice but firmer, possibly a little louder. If he tests me again, I repeat the order with a more palpable firmness, yanking his leash so he can tell I mean business. By this time, he calms down. It's almost like I've put a muzzle on my doG. At no time do I lose control and frantically yell, "*daryl*, shut up!!" If I did, it'd mean I'd given my ego power to incite me.

As I progressed training *daryl*, I became more economical with my words. I no longer needed to call him by name. I simply said, "Stop." Then I cut it to "sh." I finally got it down to not having to say anything. *daryl* will pop his head up as if wanting to bark something but I'll look at him. He'll look back at me, then put his head back down and settle into his cushion. I'm practically a doG whisperer.

Daryl Chang

I've trained my doG properly now. I, who now abide in the consciousness of my True Self, have command of my Lil-i. Lil-i waits and serves me loyally. God, my Master, is now in a position to do the work He is here to do through me. The Big-I and the Lil-i presently work as one in perfect harmony.

You might be surprised how easily you can train your doG. After a while, it doesn't bark indiscriminately. It will bark, as I mentioned earlier, if it encounters an unchecked ego. So you don't want to completely silence him. You still want him to be a doG that barks at intruders.

The sooner you get control of your ego and hand over the house keys back to the rightful owner, the sooner you will be your true self. Your well-being depends on it. An ounce of prevention is worth a pound of cure. If you get good advice and do good things, you don't have to deal with not-so-good things. If you get not-so-good advice and do not-so-good things, you'll have to deal with not-so-good things. If you control your ego, you'll be in a surplus not a deficit.

You can easily observe the behaviour of egos in society of this physical world. The battle is demonstrated in daily life of all interactions: between family members, friends, customers and staff, politicians, co-workers, et cetera.

The ego uses the same tactics internally within you, externally against those who are unconscious of who they are. A great display is with government authorities and citizens. The dark egos who are in positions of false illegitimate authority control societal rules. If you remain silent, never explicitly declining their authority but blindly comply and obey their orders, you give implied consent to them to being your master. You have denounced your sovereignty and bowed to them in slavery. So not only have you allowed your own ego to be your master, you have allowed another ego outside of you to be the master of your own ego.

Before, you had to opt-in to give consent. The dark egos flipped the game so that you now have to opt-out to say you do not give consent. Your silence gives them consent. Before, you were innocent till you were proven guilty. The dark egos flipped the game so that you are now guilty till you prove you are innocent. Your silence gives them consent to rule you guilty. Before, you were considered healthy. The dark egos flipped the game so that you are now considered sick till you prove you are healthy. Your silence gives them consent to quarantine you. Before, you were considered a good person but when you did something bad, you were punished. The dark egos flipped the game so that you are now considered a bad person but when you demonstrate you are a good person by obeying their false illegitimate orders, you are rewarded. Yes, the ego is very clever.

Your doG has power and control over you:
- If you judge, criticize, and/or condemn others.
- If you compare yourself to others, especially to make you feel good about yourself.
- If you are materialistic.
- If you are struggling with poverty.
- If you are messy and your home is cluttered.
- If you are dwelling on your past.
- If you are anxious about your future.
- If you save, accumulate, and hoard things.
- If you are struggling with your health.
- If you are struggling with a vice or an addiction.
- If you identify with anything: an object, a role, a title, et cetera.
- If you are attached to anything especially possessions or objects.
- If you have any negative emotions (ie. anger, hatred, greed, envy, resentment, et cetera).
- If you are stressed, worried, depressed, et cetera.
- If you are rushing.

I trust you see how the doG probably has control over you and can make life seem a struggle (in any capacity) without any purpose. It should be easy to see that the doG has always been in control, not just in you but many others. You have formed a prison of your own making. It is no wonder the world is in the state it is in.

The world you've created inside of yourself has extended outside of yourself. You sustain these worlds through your personal lack of consciousness.

Daryl Chang

CHAPTER 6
The Illusion of Innocence

♦

As mentioned before, much of this world doesn't make sense. All the violence, murder, and killing of one another are pure madness. Man is the only species that kills its own. We are supposedly God's greatest creation, yet we don't act as such. Alas, we are God's creations that have gone astray.

Look at bees. There are thousands of them congregated, right next to each other, cooperating together to build homes for their leader, the queen bee. Can you imagine if one bee is envious of another bee thinking the queen favours the other more? Can you imagine one bee competing with another for some title as employee bee of the month? Can you imagine if one bee got angry because it was offended that another bee invaded its space? It is evident they exist as one. Maybe they wouldn't if they did as man does.

I've seen footage of millions of ants collaborate to perform amazing feats to accomplish a task. Thousands of ants are living and working together in the life that they live as one. They don't seem to kill one another of its own kind. Even the leaves of a tree aren't foolish to try and kill the other leaves of its own tree.

I cannot think of another species that kills its own. Can you? Yes, only man does. Look around nature and it seems that man is the only foolish species to kill its own species and destroy its own habitat; the only foolish species to not naturally know it is one with itself and the rest of nature; the only foolish species to not allow God to work through them.

What is the difference between ours and other species that don't have this behaviour? Other species do not have self-consciousness equipped with an ego and free will. They are of God consciousness only and God works through them unhindered. We are a privileged species that have been give an ego and free will. You must reflect on yourself on how you contribute to this psychotic behaviour though you think you do not directly because you have not exhibited killing another.

You, who sit watching violence especially as entertainment on television but then shake your head in disbelief and disgust at others, are not good or innocent as you think you are. You, who play a violent killing video game but defend yourself that you know better than the ones who go on killing sprees and massacres, are not good or innocent as you think you are. You, who abuse another for not wearing a mask or taking a poisonous injection because you think you care more about others and humanity, are not good or innocent as you think you are.

You are unconscious of the unGod within yourself, directing your thinking, actions, and behaviour. You are easily preyed upon by other unGods, who also are unconscious of themselves, to do more of their dirty work for them indirectly. You have allowed yourself to be hijacked. You have absolved yourself of self-responsibility so that you can conveniently blame others for your own predicament and that of the world. And so the madness continues, each unconscious person sustaining the life of the unGods.

Once you recognize that you are God but you have allowed the unGod of yourself to feel the likes of anger, hatred, greed, envy, and fear to any degree, you will recognize that you have played a part in the unGodly collective acts of this world. You who have judged another are guilty and no different than the other. You are not to concern yourself of another's being and doing. You must do and become of your own accord. As Lao Tzu poignantly stated, "If you want to awaken all of humanity, then awaken all of yourself. If you want to eliminate the suffering in the world, then eliminate all that is dark and negative in yourself. Truly, the greatest gift you have to give is that of your own self-transformation." When you do, you are who you are.

God has made it very easy for us to see Him and the unGod; to know if it is Him or the unGod, the impostor.

If you feel and act with love, purity, nobility, compassion, joy, peace, calmness, and non-judgment, then you are the God that you are. If you feel right about yourself morally, then you are the God that you are. If you are experiencing peace, fortune, or well-being, then you are the God that you are.

Daryl Chang

If you feel and act with anger, hatred, frustration, greed, annoyance, envy, impurity, violence, hastiness, and judgment, then you are not the God that you are. If you feel shame, guilt, and self-hatred, then you are not the God that you are. If you judge others, you are not the God that you are. If you are competing with others, you are not the God that you are. If you are comparing yourself to others, you are not the God that you are. If you are experiencing conflict, poverty, or ill-health, then you are not the God that you are.

It is quite easy to see who you are as you think you are. You cannot fault another when the fault is yours only. God is always waiting for His prodigal son to return home. When you see it, there's no need to waste time in worrying over the past. There is still time because you are eternal and infinite. Begin now because that is all there is. Live your truth. Do not fret over others. You have your own work to do to keep you busy in this lifetime.

CHAPTER 7
Parallels

♦

All the physical world is a stage. All the physical world is a mirror. Everything is a reflection of your individual truth. All is spiritual and the physical is the spiritual manifest. God is first a spiritual and mental relation for God is spiritual mind-stuff. Hence, you are spiritual mind-stuff. The physical world is parallel to the spiritual world.

God created you but you did not create Him.

Parents give birth to children, but children do not give birth to parents. They do, however, give birth to their children, and thus give birth as their parents do. As God's creative thought proceeds from Him to you, hence your own creative thought proceeds from you to your own creations. You continue the creative process through the creative abilities within you.

Parents desire to and willingly give everything to their children. In like fashion, God desires to and willingly gives everything to you. Parents see and think their children perfect. In like fashion, God sees and thinks you and all of His creations perfect.

Parents leave all of their possessions to their children as an inheritance. In like fashion, God gives His entire kingdom to you and all of His creations. As such, know this truth. All things are already yours. When you know they are, then they are made available to you. You must understand that the principal giver of all that you need is you and your ability to receive what you want. The way to receive your desires is simply to know what you want and know you are worthy of getting it. Knowingness is the truth; it is the giver; it is your future.

You are as God, having creative ability (through thought) and creative value. If you did not have creative ability, then life would be nothing. If you did not have creative value, you would not recognize anything for what it is. That is to say, what would be the reason for the life and beauty of a flower if there were no one to appreciate its loveliness? It would have no meaning here without you.

I'd like to elaborate by giving you a practical and relatable example. God who is within me has given me the creative capability to create things. I like working with my hands. I want to create a coffee table, so I create a coffee table. The coffee table can only be appreciated if there is someone to appreciate it. God has gifted me with self-consciousness so I can appreciate the coffee table I created. God has given you the same self-consciousness to appreciate the coffee table as well. I love my coffee table but the appreciation ends there because the coffee table by its nature cannot continue creative expression. I desire to create something that can continue the proliferation of my own being. This translates into a desire to have children, who likewise can do the same. So ensues a generation to keep the creativity and creation continuing.

I am proud of my demonstration of creativity such as the coffee table I built. But the creation that gives me the most pride and joy are my children. I get to witness my expression through them as I am a part of them as they are a part of me. I receive pride and joy when I see my own children be kind, loving, and compassionate and blossom into the best human beings the world has ever seen. Others, such as friends and family, will appreciate this too.

I trust you can now see that initially God expressed His creativity by creating creations like a flower. But He desired to create a vehicle through which He could appreciate and experience His flower and all creations. He desired to continue expressing His creativity but as Himself rather than through His mere creations. And for this, He created the embodiment of man. Hence, man was created in the image and likeness of God Himself.

I trust you now firmly grasp that you are a child of God. God gave you and every other person, the totality of thought, which is the totality of Himself. God gave you a divine intelligence and a sovereign free will. Through that intelligence and freedom of will, and God within you, you have the ability to expand yourself according to your own contemplative thought processes. Thus through your own unique expression, you expand God Country.

CHAPTER 8
Consciousness

◆

I'd like to walk you through an exercise.

You are alone. Close your eyes. Think of your mom. Do you see her? How long did it take for you to see your mom? Do you see any objective time, space, and distance between you and your mom? Now pretend for a quick moment, your mom is no longer physically here on Earth anymore, as we say here, she dies. Do you see your mom? Do you see that she still exists? Do you see how she never actually dies – that she is eternal? Do you see that once you exist in consciousness, you always exist?

Think of a cashier at your local grocery store that you have yet to encounter or physically see. Does she exist? Though you have not encountered her yet, does it mean that she does not exist in Universal Consciousness?

You have to pretend or imagine this part. It's the only way because you are presently conscious of your existence now. Pretend you don't exist. Where are you? Are you are in Universal Consciousness?

Once something exists, it is in Universal Consciousness. It lives. It can be alternatively said that once something is in Universal Consciousness, it exists; it lives. Just because you don't know it exists or you are not conscious of its existence, it doesn't mean that it does not exist in Universal Consciousness. It just means you are not conscious of it yet. You exist. You are consciousness. I exist. I am consciousness. God is all in all. You and I are one with God. We are One Consciousness.

Do you see now that if you think of something, of anything, then it exists?

Do you understand now why you've heard that time, space, and distance are illusions?

Daryl Chang

Let's do another exercise. Close your eyes. Think of your mom again. If you don't happen to have one, then imagine you have the one you want. Hug each other. How do you feel? "Nice," I can hear you say. Know why? Because you are no longer separated. You are embraced as one.

In the former exercise, I asked you to pretend your mom is no longer here with us. Even though physically she is gone, you know that she existed. This is easy for you because it's your mom. If we did the same exercise for your grandparents, it'll most likely be easy as well. If we go back to your great grandparents or even further, it may be a bit intangible because most likely you've never met them in person. They physically died before you were born. But it doesn't mean they didn't exist. If you were fortunate, your grandparents might have shown you pictures. When your mom is gone but you think of her, you might say something like, "My mom is always here with me in spirit. I have her in my heart." You may have thought little of this sentiment but it is true. She is spirit.

Both exercises you ran through exemplify the sameness with God. God is the original Spirit. Though you've never met Him in person, it doesn't mean He doesn't exist. Just like your past mom, you don't necessarily need a picture of Him to identify with Him. He is the unseen formless Spirit. He is eternally here. The same can be said of Jesus. He is revered as God's begotten son because he was the one that understood, appreciated, and knew His Father. By demonstrating this, He redeemed mankind, something we should all have gratitude for.

When you embrace your spirit with our Father in your mind, your consciousness with His, you feel the same warmth and goodness because you are no longer separated from Him and realize you are one with Him. I am one with my Father, as are you.

We are all not necessarily parents but for certain we are all children. We all grow up and eventually venture out into the world to be and do something, No matter how long I've been away, when I return home to see my mom, my mom welcomes me with open arms. She is so happy to see me. I'm happy to be with her again. I'm happy when she's happy. My mom loves me. I love my mom. I admittedly disobeyed my mom in the past but she still would do anything for me. I would do anything for her as well.

It is the same with our Father. No matter your past, He forever loves you. He is always waiting for you to return home and to fully embrace you with His spiritual open arms.

I trust you can now see that you are an eternal consciousness. You, the true self, never actually die. Because you are eternal, your fear of death dissolves. The physical body you are housed in and the mask you wear are transient stages in your life. You are not separated from life. You *are* life. The physical manifestation you see in the mirror is an illusion for you to experience your human self; to physically see, appreciate, and understand your own progression toward your God self. Every thing, person, environment, and experience is there to teach and advance your self. When you are conscious of this, you may develop a habit of asking yourself what it is you are supposed to learn, particularly when you are struggling.

Just as you know you exist, know you are sitting on your couch watching a movie. You are observing the movie actors playing their roles. Your soul, the inner child, is the Observer of your human existence. You, your soul, are an unseen eternal being of consciousness, sitting in Universal Consciousness, similarly observing yourself and other characters play their part in the Greatest Masquerade Show on Earth.

Let's take a look at your needs and desires. What happens when you need something and your need is fulfilled? You don't need it anymore. What happens when you desire something and your desire is fulfilled? You no longer desire it. God has provided everything that you need and desire. Everything you need and desire is already fulfilled. You just need to know that this is true. "How is that so?" I can hear you ask.

God is all-knowing. He already knows what you need and want, so He creates and provides it. You need air to breathe. Do you need to ask for it? No, it is already here for you to use. You want water to drink? Do you need to ask for it? No, it is already here on Earth for you to have. A need or desire indicates that it already exists and is fulfilled. Let's revisit the exercise earlier where you closed your eyes and thought of your mom. As soon as you thought of her, she existed. The Principle is still working. You thought of your need for air, and it exists in Consciousness. You thought of your desire for water, and it exists in Consciousness.

It doesn't matter what the thing is. It can be a need, desire, person, object, idea, possibility, or opportunity. When you think of it, it exists. Do you see again now that if you think of something, of anything, then it exists in Consciousness?

With this in mind, you have to be cognisant that there is a time lag between your thought and the physical manifestation of it. Recall that I stated time, space, and distance are illusions. All is spiritual. In the spiritual realm, the moment you think of something, the manifestation is real. Ideally, the manifestation is instantaneous in the physical realm as you wish or so you'd like to think. If you inadvertently had a negative thought, you'd be glad that it wasn't instantaneous – you presently have the grace of time to correct your thoughts. However, in your present unpractised stage of evolution, you have yet to master this. The manifestation is real but your physical experience of it is not immediate. The time of your experience is unspecified. It may be minutes, hours, days, months, or years but it is certain if your thought process is proper. You must accept and know this to be true. If you doubt, worry, or lack faith, then the process is broken.

Now that you know that all your needs and desires are met, it should make sense to you that you shouldn't *really* have any human needs or desires anymore. Physical desires are generally from the ego of your limited human mind because he thinks he is separate from God. The ego is attached to it because he can identify with it. As such, he exceedingly wants it. When you notice a desire within you but you are not attached to it (ie. you aren't bothered whether you get it or not), then it's a good possibility that it's God speaking to you. The desire He put in you may be integral to the progression of your full expression. You don't have longing for it and are not attached to it because you know you have everything fulfilled already. If God means for you to have it to serve your purpose, then you will have it.

Know that the human mind thinks; the God Mind KNOWS.

Knowing something is a great feeling. Knowing is so much better than not knowing, assuming, believing, and guessing. When you know it, you feel and experience it throughout your body. You can talk about romantic love intellectually but if you haven't felt and experienced it, then you still don't know. When you know something and feel it, consciousness takes you there where it's real. Knowing is the emotional ascertainment of the thing. A desire is nothing more than the thought of fulfillment seen through an object, entity, or experience. So if you think of a thing you desire, though the physical realization may not be there at the moment instantly as you wish, know with absolute certainty that it is fulfilled. You'll be filled with joy. This is how God works.

All the things I've described up to this point cumulatively add up to another insightful moment. Yet again, something simple yet unfathomable just needs to be accepted as true. I'll take a pause here so you can let what you've read so far truly sink in. Reread it if you'd like. I'll wait for you.

Okay, how great is this? God is all in all. God is Consciousness. Consciousness is in everything. I am consciousness. Everything, down to the cell, is consciousness. It's in the cells of my own body, the houseplant, and the sun. And because all is One, you can speak to any single consciousness as its God self. That single consciousness will respond to you in kind because you are one with it.

Whatever I think, say, or do to someone or something, I think, say, and do to myself. Whatever I think, say, or do to myself, I think, say, or do to someone or something. If it's not a person but an object, say a houseplant or my foot, I personify it to make it more substantial and perceptible, and speak to it as I would a personal friend. Since the cells are consciousness, they will hear me. If it needs healing and I bring that intention when I speak to it, it will restore itself to its perfect God self as it is. You know this more commonly as prayer.

CHAPTER 9
The Personification
of God

♦

I notice that the more removed you are from your spirituality, the more you must relate to everything from a physical perspective. You have been accustomed to embrace reality only from that which you can experience with your physical senses. You must be able to identify in physical terms that which you do not understand. Inherently, it must make logical sense. You must be satisfied intellectually before you allow any further personal growth; progress beyond where you are, especially spiritually, is not possible. All is incomprehensible otherwise.

Just as you will admit you are a living organism, every "thing" is an organism. The universe is a living organism. The solar system is a living organism. The planet is a living organism. The human and any other being of nature is a living organism. The cell is a living organism. The atom is a living organism.

You are a planet. The physical planet you call your body is a perfect example of the totality of God.

Within your living being, you are connected by your body parts that serve your whole being. You have given names to all the individual parts from the largest to the miniscule. You've given them labels such as the liver, kidneys, lungs, heart, brain, arms, legs, red blood cells, and white blood cells. Each cell has intelligence, collaborates and serves every other cell. All naturally cooperate for the higher good of the body, the human, and the soul it lives within.

An organ, say your liver, within you would not intentionally harm the being, you, that contains it for that would mean its own death. Conversely, you would not intentionally hurt or cut off one of your own living parts, say your arm, because you are conscious though it is not the whole of you, that it is a part of you and that it serves you.

God is all in all. God is every thing. Whereas you – *man* – are the human personality, God is the Divine Impersonality. Whereas you think, act, and take things personally, God thinks, acts, and takes things impersonally. God acts impersonally with equal willingness toward the saintly good person or the devious bad person just as the sun would keenly shine on either.

God is a *faceless* living organism. Every "thing" is a part of God and is connected to its entire Being. You are a cell of God's body.

Similar to your own person, God has many parts, of which you are one. The entire universe is God's body. Humanity is God's Body. The living planet you call Earth is part of His Body. For instance, you can consider water circulating His system as you would your blood; continents as His organs, the trees as His lungs, and all human beings as white blood cells circulating and serving His entire Being. No thing of nature would intentionally harm God, the Being that holds all of them. Conversely, God would not want to intentionally hurt or cut off one of His own living parts that are there to serve His whole being.

Humans have been blessed with a unique consciousness unlike much of nature, for its existence. The human being, a servant cell organism of God, has the ability to serve its Master as he should. However, through a lack of consciousness, he has the capacity to destroy its Master.

Unfortunately, many persons of mankind are unconscious of who they are. The human being has become the hand that is not aware of itself beyond itself, its function, and unknowingly destroys its own whole being.

The collective human consciousness observed today is unconscious that hurting the planet is hurting himself. The collective human consciousness is unconscious that hurting his fellow human being is hurting himself. The collective human consciousness is unconscious that everything is connected. The collective human consciousness must raise its level of consciousness to remember the connectedness, the oneness and the totality of creation itself; and the true nature and purpose of itself.

Daryl Chang

Each individual of that collective who remains unconscious is like the cancer cell within his or her own body that must evolve into a healthy one, otherwise it contributes to destroying its own host. Unless you hand over all your intelligence and power to Him, the All-Knowing, for the purpose of expressing Himself, the result is imperfect functioning. This disharmony is evident in its effects of war, poverty, dis-ease, suffering, death, et cetera, individually and collectively. These are the factual dis-eases of humanity.

When more persons are conscious of who they are, they function as healthy cells. They change the terrain; the environment; the collective human consciousness. We are all One Mind so each one who advances influences others. The consciousness of the unconscious souls will be unconsciously transformed. The elevation of consciousness contributes to the restoration of God Country.

I trust the aforesaid gives you a clearer perspective and that you now see the totality and oneness of God that extends beyond yourself. When you become conscious of who you are, you know you are more than a mere human being. God is within you; you are a part and an extension of God. When you begin to see the Oneness of life, *God*, any ugliness evaporates. You begin to see life as a game of practice where you strive to establish goodness in your own character, as well as in the world. You will collaborate, cooperate, and serve others for the sake of all existence. All cooperate for the highest good of God and all of nature.

CHAPTER 10
Oneness

♦

The linear mind says it's this or that. It can't be that because it's this. If it's this, then it can't be that. The non-linear mind says it's this and that. It's both. Say what? God is all in all. This is the irony or nature of Oneness.

Oneness is simply the idea, God is. And in his Being, He encompasses all things.

Oneness is the essence of existence of something, of anything, of everything.

From Oneness, all things are connected. In that sense, oneness and connectedness mean the same.

Oneness is a We/Us-mentality because you recognize that we are all connected to that oneness.

Connectedness is the unity of all things. It is the feeling and consciousness of participating in something greater than Oneself, yet which also is Oneself. In ecology, this is the principle of interdependence: that all beings depend for their survival on the web of other beings that surround them, ultimately extending out to encompass the entire planet.

Duality and dissection of any degree is a human fragmentation or shattering of oneness. All such forms disguise Oneness by creating and increasing separation.

Duality is a human mental construct. Duality is a necessary tool for discernment. For example, you cannot understand or appreciate joy without sorrow. With partial consciousness, it is the sorrow that propels you towards joy. With full consciousness and recognition of oneness, it is the joy that eventually becomes your natural state with sorrow unknown.

Separation is a You/Them-mentality. Separation is the confusion of all things. It is the lack of consciousness of your Oneself and the Oneness of creation. It is the lack of recognition on the interdependence that exists with all. The extinction of any species, including our own, diminishes our own wholeness, our own health, our own selves; something of our very being is lost.

Your mind and the mind of God are One.

To be one is to be of one mind and will. When your will and mind, and God's will and mind are one, then you will understand the mystique of God, love, and truth. Recognizing and understanding Oneness positions you to recognize yourself in another; to embrace the "good" and the "bad" within yourself and others; to act virtuously.

By acknowledging this, you become fully aware of your Creator. All sense of separation disappears. This establishes the peace of God. If you perceive truly, you are cancelling out misperceptions in yourself and others simultaneously. Because you see them as they truly are, you offer them your acceptance of their truth so they can accept it for themselves. This is the healing that love induces.

As I mentioned earlier, if you are removed from your spirituality, you must relate to everything from a physical perspective. It must make logical sense to you. Otherwise, all is incomprehensible. Perhaps you feel the aforementioned is pretentious blather. If it's unclear to you, I'll try to make it more relatable as follows.

Let's take a two-dollar coin we endearingly call a twoonie. Pull one out from your pocket if you have it. It might help as I go along here. There are two sides. You call one side "heads". You call its counterpart on the other side "tails". Put the coin on the table with the heads up. Right now, you see heads only. You wouldn't know tails exist on the flip side if you never flip it. You would think that particular side is all there is to the coin – just the one side, in this case, heads. Same thing goes if you have the tails side up instead.

If you position the coin balanced vertically on its tip, and you look straight on, you'd see what amounts to be a vertical line. You would not necessarily be aware of the two sides existing.

This example is to emphasize how you deliberately call one side heads and the other tails to separate and identify the two but you perceive or know that it is one coin. For practical purposes, you will admit that you never identify with just heads or tails alone. You see it as one coin.

Let's take a look at an apple. Go get one if you'd like. An apple being round doesn't have evident sides such that we could differentiate a left or right side. Take a knife and slice it down the middle. Just like the coin, you can now label one half something and the other half as something else, say the good half and the bad half. You can keep cutting multiple pieces out of the apple and give each one a name. Note, this is what man and science does. They keep cutting and separating everything. If you keep separating yourself from another and every thing around you, you are increasingly separating yourself from God. You become UnGod.

If you give a slice of the apple to a friend and ask him "What is it?" what do you think his answer would be? I'm certain your friend would recognize it and say it's an apple. Would you agree? Although the slice is separate from the whole apple, you wouldn't identify it as a left or right side of the apple. You and he recognize that it is still a part of the "one" apple and so you both call it an apple.

Let's take a look at your brain. I'm sure you've heard that your brain has two parts, the left-brain and the right-brain. One side is not judged "good" and the other "bad". The left-brain has its functions and is mainly identified as being analytical and logical. The right-brain has its functions and is mainly identified with creativity and intuition. They are both equally vital in the whole of the brain, and it is stated that brain function is optimal when both left and right sides are working in balanced cohesion. You recognize that the whole is greater than the sum of its parts.

Let's take a look at your own oneness as a "human being". I've identified earlier that you have a true self and a false self. Traditionally, you might have heard most people just say you had an ego and a self. But the labels used are not the point here. The point is you can keep separating parts of you and identifying them with names, but those parts are not the whole of you. In the end, you are just one person.

By now, I trust that you understand Oneness, God, and the totality of everything in the universe. I am one with God. You are one with God. All of us are one. When you are vigilant of who you are, you will become more conscious of this all the time. When you begin to see no thing as separate, that all things are in a flow of Oneness, you will begin to become and act as God is and does. Always bring the thought to one purpose, one action, one Principle. When you see life in this way, all unpleasantness vanishes.

Oneness is demonstrated and easily seen in all that we do and say. Here are some examples for your consideration.
- You think so you exist; you exist so you think.
- You teach what you want to learn; you learn what you want to teach.
- You want a girl to love; you want to love a girl.
- You eat to live; you live to eat.
- You are active to be healthy; you are healthy because you are active.
- You grow old because you stop playing; you stop playing because you grow old.
- You smile because you are in joy; you are in joy because you smile.
- You sing because you are happy; you are happy because you sing.
- Miracles happen because you believe in them; you believe in miracles because they happen.
- Which came first, the chicken or the egg?
- Which came first, the seed or the plant?
- Which came first: the thought or the words?
- Are your thoughts determined and formed by your vocabulary or does your vocabulary determine and form your thoughts?

Take a point. Expand the point. You now have a line. The line seemingly has two opposites. Bring these opposites together. You now have a circle. The opposites are no more. Expand the circle. You now have a perfect sphere. You have completed a synchronized relationship of all elements. The point becomes the line, the line becomes the circle, and the circle becomes the sphere. The sphere is the cosmos or universe.

This is true of every *line* of thought. Through the continuous process of relating all things to the One instead of separating every thing, the point of unity or oneness is established. This is One-pointedness. This is Oneness.

God is all in all. God is One. It is all a spiritual realm. When you become fully conscious to see it as it truly it is, who you are and your part in it, the Cosmos is one universal plane working in perfect unison with itself. This is harmonious thought. Your consciousness of Consciousness is spiritual influence which permeates all time and space and in which they work.

There is only one God and God is all in all. That what is not God is not the opposite. It is simply less of God that requires correction. For example, there is no good or evil (ie. when you use them to deem them opposites). This seems like wordplay and it is but it is your belief in opposites that impedes your progress. There is nothing either good or evil, but the thinking makes it so. I can hear the doubters, haters, and freedom fighters right now saying, "Here's another guy spewing New Age bullshit." It's not New Age. In fact, it's Old Age.

When someone of limited thinking does not understand or know something, they say it is stupid. Their egos are in play. Their doGs are barking. They are of low consciousness, unacquainted with themselves. The doG is trying to assert itself as God and so if other doGs are listening, they too will bark and howl alongside. But God the Master will order, "doG, be quiet," and the doG shall obey.

There is nothing good or evil because God is good only. To believe or say this or that is evil is to believe or say God is evil which He is not. What is considered evil destroys itself by its own nature yet it contains the seed or germ of good. It is better to view that which you perceive as evil as less good, or simply as not good.

The intellect is the child of the limited human mind. To say that there is nothing evil sounds silly. The current world contains the likes of tyrants, murderers, and pedophiles, and the intellectual mind deems these evil. "Do you mean to say that we shall accept them all and call them good?" I can hear you ask. They are included in the providence and the life and the wonderment of God. God is all in all. Each ego involved in the evil act, say murder, played its part for the resulting experience. It is only your human ego looking from the outside that is judging it good or

Daryl Chang

evil. Those within the experience needed it for their evolution. If you abhor the act and place judgment on the "evil" person, you have placed it upon yourself. You will be affected by that judgment for you will have taken a part of itself and separated from your being. Then you are no longer whole. You are a contradiction of God. Do not abhor the act. Reason it. Understand it. Go beyond it.

The evil you see and despise is in a collective mirror and serves as an impetus. You must likewise look at your own individual mirror to declare that it is in you as well. How would you recognize it otherwise? It is a lesson to teach you to turn to yourself, God within. You must see it for what it really is – a force permitted by God to try, test, and develop your strength of character and to teach you wisdom; to teach you who you are.

The evil is a part of you and it isn't a part of you. It allows you to discern what is not you so that you can know what is you. Once you know both, then you know One, and then you know to know only One: *God*. Evil cannot hurt you when you know who you are – *God*, love. Your love dispels the evil that you judge with your limited human mind. When you know this, you need only be the love that you are, stand aside and watch God work, realizing that in time evil will destroy itself.

If this does not make sense to you at this present point here, it is indicating that you are still thinking with your limited human mind, your logical reasoning mind. The mind, intellect, or reason will not allow you to see or understand this. Reason knows neither principle nor morality. Your reason is like a lawyer in that it will argue for either side.

The intellect of a thief will plan a robbery and murder as readily as the intellect of a saint will plan a great philanthropy. Intellect helps us to see the best means and manner of doing the right thing but intellect never shows us the right thing. Intellect and reason serve the selfish man for his selfish ends as readily as they serve the unselfish man for his unselfish ends.

This is the irony of your divinity, of trying to analyze who you are. It is only necessary that you accept that you are God and that we are all One with no negative thoughts or statements regarding it.

Oftentimes, you must trust the process though it doesn't make sense to your intellect. This is akin to airplanes. The world never accepted it as a possibility until it actually flew. Now that we can fly, there are infinite intellectual explanations as to how and why it is so. If bees had man's limited thinking, they would not fly. Facts come first and then accounted for later.

CHAPTER 11
Only One

♦

The ego, the unGod and the human being of your false self, thinks he is separate from One and all. Man who is presently ruled by the UnGod cuts, slices, and unendingly separates every thing. In his lack of consciousness, understanding, and belief of God and who he is, he ironically does this to try and understand God and himself. He naively does not think to go directly to the Source: *God*.

The separation of One into many things is that of Man. The recognition and acknowledgement of only One is that of *God*.

There is not man and God. There is only One – *God*.

There is not mankind. There is only One – *God*.

There are not humans, birds, fish, livestock, wild animals, and creatures that move along the ground. There is only One – *God*.

There are many masks worn. There is only one identity – *God*.

There is not a Conscious, Subconscious, and Superconscious Mind. There is only One Mind – *God*.

There is not physical and spiritual. There is only spiritual – *God*.

There are not multiple laws as man has made up to explain the universe. There is no law of attraction, law of karma, law of least effort, et cetera. There are many illegitimate man-made laws. There is only one law – *God*.

There is not good and evil. There is only good – *God*.

There are not many undesirable states (ie. poverty, dis-ease, war, et cetera). There is only one state – *God*.

There are not many different type of loves. There is not phileo, storge, eros, and agape. There is only one love – *God*.

There are many illusions. There are not many realities. There is only one reality – *God*.

There are not many problems. There is only one problem – that of separation from *God*.

There are many questions. There is only one answer – *God* (love).

There are not many solutions. There is only one solution – *God*.

CHAPTER 12
Space

♦

There is famous parable about six blind men and an elephant. The story goes like this. Six blind men try to learn what an elephant is like by touching it. The first blind man touched the side, felt it smooth and solid, so he said it was like a wall. The second blind man held the trunk and announced it was like a snake. The third blind man felt the tusk and decided it was sharp and deadly like a spear. The fourth blind man touched one of the elephant's four legs and said it was like a pillar. The fifth blind man felt the elephant's ear and stated it was like a huge fan or magic carpet. The sixth blind man held the coarse tail and declared it was like a rope. The six blind men loudly argued with each other over who was right.

The moral of the parable is that humans have a tendency to claim absolute truth based on their limited mind and experience.

I'd like to delve into another aspect of this story.

When you look up into an incredibly dark sky, you marvel at the stars. Most likely, you never think to marvel at the space between the stars. You think of it as nothing. If there was no space between things, there would be no form to discern. In the light of day that fills the sky and space, you are oblivious to the stars that exist still above. Space is the power that holds everything.

I'd like to walk you through an exercise.

Remember the coffee table I built earlier. I made it three feet by three feet square and painted it a dark brown colour. I blindfold you. I lead you to it and have you place your face at the centre, two inches from the surface so that you're looking directly at a dark brown one inch square. I remove your blindfold. Pretend for a moment you are not aware of my coffee table as I've just described. I ask, "Can you tell me what you're looking at?" "I don't know," I can hear you say. I blindfold you again and then lead you standing six feet away from the table. I remove the blindfold. I now ask, "Can you tell me what you're looking at?" "A coffee table," I can hear you say.

The first time I asked you to identify the object, you had a limited view of it so you didn't know what it was. The second time when I asked the question, you identified it. There was space around the form. You had a higher viewpoint and greater perspective.

Let's run through another exercise.

I blindfold you. I lead you to your mom and guide your face to the centre of her palm, once inch from the surface so that you're looking directly at a one inch square patch of skin. I remove your blindfold. I ask, "Can you tell me what you're looking at?" "I don't know," I can hear you say. I blindfold you again and then lead you six inches away from her hand. I remove the blindfold. I now ask, "Can you tell me what you're looking at?" "A hand," I can hear you say. "But whose hand?" I ask. "I don't know," I can hear you say. I blindfold you once more. I lead you six feet away from your mom. I remove your blindfold. I ask, "Whose hand is it?" "It's my mom's hand," I can hear you say.

The first time I asked you to identify the object, you had a limited view of it so you didn't know what it was. The second time when I asked the question, you identified the hand. There was space around the form. You had a higher viewpoint and greater perspective. But you could not recognize whose it was. The third time when I asked you whose hand it was, you identified your mom. You had an even higher viewpoint and even greater perspective.

Let's say I ran through a similar exercise in nature. I lead you to a one inch square of the bark of a tree. Most likely, you wouldn't be able to identify it. I lead you say ten feet away. Then you're able to identify the tree of which prior you only spotted a section of its bark. I finally lead you one hundred thousand feet above the sky, beyond the planet, into the vastness of the universe where there is much space. You now have a higher viewpoint and greater perspective you did not have moments ago. Only then is there the possibility that you see the tree as a body part of God, a lung of His.

For the above exercises, you used your sense of physical sight. Now let's follow an exercise using your sense of physical hearing.

Daryl Chang

You and I are in a crowded café enjoying a beverage. I have you hold a baby in your arms while I have a conversation with you. I ask you, "Can you hear the baby's heartbeat?" "No," I can hear you say. We return home where there's more quiet and sit relaxed on the sofa. I have you hold the baby's chest next to your ear but continue talking to you. I ask, "Can you hear the baby's heartbeat?" "No," I can hear you say. I leave the room so that you are in solitude with the baby. I return and ask, "Did you hear the baby's heartbeat?" "Yes," I can hear you say.

What is exemplified as true for your physical senses is equally true for your spiritual senses.

Only when there is finally a space between the constant noise around can you hear the sounds that were once inaudible. And so it must be to hear and experience the voice of God. This world is filled with incessant noise throughout your busy daily life. You have never paused to determine who you really are. You have not been aware that the human personality that you forever thought you were is not your true self. You have been completely unaware of God's presence. When you do not set yourself still, you will never know of Him and hear the deep silent small voice within. Still yourself, listen with your spiritual ears and you will hear His voice. Your ego and intellect will scoff at this and reject this as nonsense. It doesn't want you entertaining the idea of this experience for it knows it may mean the beginning of its demise.

When you look at a physical human being with your physical eyes and limited human mind, you see a physical face. When you look beyond the physical face to that which has no physical features, there is a non-physical space where you see a human personality. This has been your habit for a long time now. When personalities clash, conflict ensues. You can establish a newer and better habit. When you go further beyond this human personality, there is yet another non-physical space below this human personality. When you look at this space as you can only with your loving spiritual eyes and unlimited divine mind, you look past the distractions of the physical form and human personality. You will see an invisible formless divine soul that is pure and perfect. Unlike the various human personalities, this entity is the same across all divine beings beneath the human masks worn.

Again, your ego and intellect will ridicule you for wanting to change your habits. It doesn't want you entertaining the idea. It knows that you may be pleasantly surprised from this experience where love and peace lie. Its life is severely threatened even more from such a practice.

God is all in all. Universal Consciousness is in everything, so it must fill all space too. In fact, it is space or that which we call space. God is the visible form manifest. But God is also the invisible formless unmanifest. He is the space. Space is the unseen invisible unmanifest from which comes the power of creation: *God.* Space allows you to witness all creations; from you to all of nature.

You may think of space as nothing not knowing it is everything. Space which you think of as nothing is the invisible formless unmanifest from which everything becomes visible form manifest. Space is the formless that gives form its power. It is space that allows the spiritual senses to activate and override the physical senses. It is space that embodies the essence of form. It is space that provides the emptiness to see true form. It is space that provides the silence to hear the voice of God within.

CHAPTER 13
Spiritual Beginnings,
Physical Endings

♦

Have you ever baked a cake? I have. I'd like to walk you through the process.

Initially, I have no idea what cake I want to make. So I look through recipes till I see one created by someone with a picture of the final product that appeals to me. When I do, I mentally say, "Yes, that's the cake I want to make." I read through the ingredients needed. I have a mental thought of the ingredients I need to get. I go to the grocery to get the physical ingredients. I come home. I prepare the tools and ingredients I mentally know I need and put them on the physical counter. I run through the baking instructions. I follow the instructions step by step by the person who created the recipe. When the cake is done, I look at it. It's exactly like the picture I saw earlier at the beginning before I even had physical proof I could do it.

Now, let's say I saw the recipe and saw the picture but didn't read through the ingredient list or the instructions. Instead, even though I have limited knowledge on making it, I'm a bit full of myself and think I can make it without those tedious instructions. I figure I'd try. I get the ingredients I thought I needed (aka, I'm guessing). I run through some procedure I thought would produce the pictured cake (aka, I'm guessing). It wouldn't come out like the picture.

Because I really want to make this cake, I try again. It still doesn't come out perfect but I'm highly motivated so I keep trying. I may eventually get it or not. Wouldn't it be easier and wiser to get directions from the creator of the recipe and simply follow their instructions? This way, I wouldn't have to burden myself with trying to figure it out on my own. All I need to know is what I want and leave the how to the creator.

Let's briefly recap the two scenarios above. In the first one, I decided what I wanted and pictured it mentally. Then I followed the directions I got from the creator of the recipe who knows how to do it. During the different stages of the entire process, the things I needed physically were received. I didn't think about how to do it. I listened to the recipe instructions step by step and eventually, I produced the final physical product.

In the second one, I decided what I wanted and pictured it mentally. Then I didn't follow the directions I got from the creator of the recipe who knows how to do it. Instead, I tried to figure it out on my own and did what I thought was right. During the different stages of the entire process, some of the things I thought I needed physically were received but not completely. If I was honest with myself, I'd admit I didn't really know what I was doing and wished someone had just told me how. Through my own limited and perverted thinking do I mess up the resulting cake for an otherwise perfect recipe.

Let's see if I can relate these principles to life in general. First, if I decide what I want and picture it mentally with joy and enthusiasm over the thought of the final product; then if I check my ego so that I recognize I don't have to figure out things on my own; then if I simply follow directions from the Creator God; eventually, what I want will manifest. In brief, the 'what' is my job. The 'how' is God's.

God is the Power, the Intelligence, the All-Knowing who works through me. I am the Observer. I am the baker who follows the recipe in which He provides the instructions. I do not question the directions. He has done all the creative work already in how the final product is completed. I just need to hear His instructions and execute them. When I'm done, I subsequently enjoy the cake. I can have my cake and eat it too.

In the second scenario of the prior example, I do not start at the bottom: *the cake*. I do not cut the cake into a gazillion pieces to figure out what the cake is made of (ie. the ingredients) and how to make it. No, I start from the very top and work my way down. The result is the cake. I just have to appreciate and enjoy the cake after.

An architect always produces a blueprint first before the physical house is built. The design and all its specifications are first thought of in the unseen spiritual world. When this is clear, then the physical development occurs – the materials, the machinery, the workers, et cetera to produce the house that reflects the blueprint. If the house requires changes like a new addition, the process is repeated. That is, workers do not begin by tackling it by physical means first. They do not start by physically renovating parts indiscriminately. They do not know what the final product is that they are working toward. The architect has to produce another blueprint in his thoughts first, the unseen world, for the desired renovation.

When you want to create anything, you do not start at the bottom: *the something*. You do not cut the something into a gazillion pieces to figure what the something is made of and how to make it. No. To make it, you start at the very top. You go to the spiritual world first. You think and see what you want; you go to the Source: *God*; and you follow His direction to create the something.

All is spiritual first; all things physical are spiritual made manifest. The spiritual is the unseen formless inner *causative* realm and the physical is the visible formed outer *effectual* realm. That is, the life you are experiencing physically ("good" or "bad") is simply evidence, showing you what you have cumulatively created in your spiritual world. Your spiritual world stems from your Being, which is impacted by your mental and emotional state of being. When you have an undesired physical issue or experience you would like to resolve, know you must be rooted in the simple joy of Being first instead of solely doing. That is, focus on the joy of Being and do not lose your self in just doing, especially a role. Be, then do. You will be more efficient and productive adjusting your thoughts rather than tackling them through physical means.

Man (ego) has overly cultivated the intellect. He has gone to the extreme and dismissed his spirituality. In this present day, he is absolutely fixated on the physical world only. Earlier, I indicated that the physical world is parallel to the spiritual world. The physical realm is merely reflecting what has occurred in the spiritual realm.

Somewhere along the way, the original gods forgot who they were and got seduced by their own creations. The initial gods were love so they created, appreciated, and repeated. Their creations of man must have let their egos slip as it is today. They started competing with each other, forgetting they did not need to and that they were not supposed to. They could all create agreeably alongside each other but they soon forgot this and started to go astray till they were utterly lost. Because they were lost, they had to find their way back home. They forgot about their Source, *God*. They started working backward trying to figure out how what they created was created. They started cutting, slicing and dicing, relentlessly separating parts, trying to guess what the elements were and how it was made. They became highly mental; they overly cultivated the intellect; and they cut off their spirituality. They foolishly did not think to just go to the Source – *God* – and work top down. Their limited human minds had betrayed them. You know this more commonly as what is termed "science".

If you truly reflect, you will admit that science always keeps changing and needs revising because it knows not much really. It is only based upon conjecture or theory. It is not absolute because it is man in his limited thinking. There is no true science, religion, law, medicine, social structure, or any other concept the UnGod has invented. In all this time, you should ask yourself, "Why do I blindly construe "science" as affirmative? Why am I so easily deceived by the claims of the big unGods when they say science says this or that? Why do I accept their manipulations as truth? Why do I no longer question whatever they state as truth? Why do I so readily accept their beliefs and truths as my own? Why have I become this way?"

The kingdom of God is first spiritual; is within. The physical evidence will display when firmly established in the spiritual.

So here we are today. The souls that are most lost and disconnected – the dark egos, the big unGods, the big doGs – are trying to create a false kingdom for their own selfish purposes: humans that can be forever their slaves. For you to be their ultimate slave, you need to be like the coffee table. They neither want you to be able to think nor create yourselves to serve others. They want you to exist only to serve them for their own appreciation and enjoyment. They want some of the human capabilities but only the parts that serve them well.

The big unGods cannot start at the very top, the Source: *God*, because God is God and they are not. So, they started at the bottom: *the human*. They cut a human into a gazillion pieces to figure what he is made of and how he is made. With the current technology and limited knowledge they have, they try to remove God who is within you so that they can take His place. They want to build thinkless and emotionless irobots to serve their dystopian world.

Daryl Chang

The big unGods do not need or want you "doing" anything. Instead, they need and want you "being" in fear. You are a fear factory self-generating fear, their most precious and renewable energy resource. You voluntarily provide this for them because you are unconscious of who you are. All is spiritual; the physical is spiritual manifest. The big unGods imprison your mind. Consequently, you are physically imprisoned in cages with invisible walls. Their tactics consist of locking you down in your home; restricting your movement anywhere; and incessantly monitoring and tracking your whereabouts. They are enslaving you who are unconscious of the true God within. You have been hypnotized to blindly obey and comply.

I recall somewhere the definition of illusion is that which is ever changing. Conversely, reality is that which does not. The physical realm provides evidence for your life. What you see and experience is perpetually changing, hence an illusion. This unGodly world that seems to be a reality is an illusion. God (love) is unwavering, immutable, beneficent, and real. God Country is the true reality. God is the only reality.

The big unGods have choreographed an illusion in which you are still contributing because of your unconsciousness. That is, you do not remember who you are thereby allowing them to hijack your mind. This unGodly world will collapse when you regain full consciousness of who you are.

I cite the Course in Miracles that states: "Nothing real is ever threatened. Nothing unreal exists. Therein lies the peace of God."

CHAPTER 14
Flow

♦

God is all in all. God is One. I am God, you are God, and so on. When you love God, you love yourself. When you love yourself, you love God. God is giving and receiving unto itself. God is a dynamic, moving, ever-flowing force. If this flow of force is restricted or hampered, then its power will become stagnant and reduced toward death.

I have always innately desired to release whatever is within me, such as knowledge, love, joy, and peace to others. It feels good when I do. I am certain that if you paused to reflect on yourself, you would admit this too. This release is essential and should not be restrained.

The thoughts I have, whether they be negative or positive, must be released. I release my thoughts by talking to someone, saying it out loud, or writing them on paper. If I do not release my thoughts, it can result in mental clutter, disorder, chaos, and confusion. My entire being is affected. If I release my thoughts, it can result in mental clarity, peace, and intelligence. My entire being is affected. I have permitted flow.

The feelings I have, whether they be negative or positive, must be released somehow. I release my feelings by crying, smiling, or laughing. If I do not release my feelings, it can result in discomfort, pain, and illness. My entire being is affected. If I release my feelings, it can result in comfort, pleasure, and well-being. I feel relief, lightness, and peace. The feelings I release will multiply. I have permitted flow.

Note that in the aforesaid, negative thoughts and feelings should not be released directly as such. If negative thoughts and feelings such as fear, anger, and hatred are released immediately, they too will multiply on their own. You know this. If you project your fear, lash out in anger, or act out your hatred, then you generate more fear, anger, and hatred, not just in yourself but others if they too are unconscious. You do not feel good after such release. You do not feel relief, lightness, or peace. In fact, you feel stressed, heavy, and conflicted. Would you agree?

Negative thoughts and feelings must first be transmuted to positive ones before being released. You must transmute them as love, joy, and peace. "How do I transmute my negative thoughts and feelings?" I can hear you ask. You put it through the love machine: *God*.

Have you ever seen a pasta or noodle maker? You feed your unappealing blob of dough through it and it produces refined noodles. Have you ever seen a wood chipper? You feed your large rough pieces of wood through it and it produces these refined woodchips. Have you ever built a campfire? You place your coarse logs in a fire and it eventually produces refined ash. Your love machine will work similarly. You feed your dreadful, repulsive negative thoughts and feelings through it, and it produces refined tender loving ones.

Your love machine is a personally customized virtual device that comes with a lifetime guarantee. You spiritually design in your mind, a noodle maker, a wood chipper, or a fireplace of sorts, however you like and whatever works for you. Situate it in a place within yourself like you would your favourite espresso machine on your kitchen counter because you know you regularly use it; where it is readily available and accessible; where it is visible and can't be missed. When it is visible in your consciousness like your espresso machine, you will use it because you know when you do, you get great pleasure and satisfaction from the end product.

God is the breath of life, for breath is life. Breath is essential to life. Breath is energy, substance, and intelligence. The act of breathing exemplifies the dynamic, moving, and ever-flowing force that God is.

You can inhale and then try to hold your breath. If your breathing was absolutely restricted, intentional or not, you would eventually die. You will admit that at some point, you have to exhale to allow your breath to flow again. You feel alive again when you do. There is a steady in and out, a giving and receiving dynamic that is a necessary part to continuous life. This natural principle applies to all aspects of your being. Whether it is love, kindness knowledge, money, time, food, et cetera, it must keep flowing like the act of breathing. If you hoard what you possess, your life will become stagnant. By ensuring its continuous flow, you ensure the flow returns to you in kind, thereby enriching you.

Giving and receiving are one of the same. When you give to others, you give to yourself. When you give to yourself, you give to others. When you are willing to receive what you are willing to give, and when you are willing to give what you are willing to receive, then you understand love: *God.*

You naturally know this though you may not have ever reflected on it. When someone does not receive well a gift you want to fully give, even something as a simple compliment that's deflected or dismissed through some false humility or undeserved feeling, you feel rejected and dejected. Would you agree? Giving and receiving are the same, and are of equal significance. You cannot give if another does not receive and you cannot receive if another does not give.

This unGodly society has conditioned you to save, collect, and accumulate a myriad of things for which they have defined value for you – money, stamps, coins, sports cards, magnets, points, hits, likes, viewers, followers, et cetera. You have become addicted to the apparent approval you gain from others for having them. You have been deceived that there is scarcity and that you must compete with others to ensure you get and keep your share. You have been misled to be and act with this poverty mindset in order to survive.

Because you are unconscious of who you are, you believe and accept this as life. You are mistaken. This behaviour is contrary to the flow of God. You are made to give and receive, and allow God to dynamically flow through you. You are a child of God and He has provided everything to you and everyone. Your unconsciousness puts you in fear. Your consciousness restores your love.

The intellectual linear mind thinks that once you give something, you have lost it; that you no longer have it. That giving and receiving is one seems counterintuitive but it is quite a remarkable mechanism. Let me elaborate.

If I take a physical object and I give it to you and you receive it, I no longer have it. I give you $1. You receive it. I no longer have the $1. You now have $1. I give you a cake. You receive the cake. I no longer have the cake. You now have a cake. I give you one hour of time to help you move furniture. You receive it. I no longer have one hour I had before. You now have one hour of time of another to help move your furniture.

However, if I give you that which is not physical but that which is spiritual, it comes back to me as if I never gave it.

I give you $1. You receive it. It brings me joy to help you financially – that is, I receive joy. You have joy because you are able to use $1 to buy the car you desired. I give you cake. You receive it. It brings me joy to bake something delicious for you to eat – that is, I receive joy. You have joy because you found it tasty and it satisfied your hunger. I give you one hour of time. You receive it. It brings me joy to help you – that is, I receive joy. You have joy because your home is now arranged in the way you want. I gave and I received. You received. You gave.

The divine Flow Principle is working. The physical act of having given but not received is an illusion. All things are spiritual. The physical is spiritual manifest. The giving of the $1, cake, and time were the manifested physical human experiences of giving. The law of God is immutable. There is just a time lag which doesn't provide instant gratification or physical evidence of the full exchange yet. The flow is happening. The higher power and intelligence is working. At some point in time, I receive the $1, the cake, and the time back not linearly or necessarily equivalent as $1, cake, or time, but categorically as some form of abundance.

I trust you now see that the things you should want are the things you can give away without losing – *the spiritual*. The things you shouldn't exceedingly want are the things you can lose – *the physical*. As I've said frequently, all is spiritual; the physical is spiritual manifest. So the physical will be received in time. Spiritual currencies are the true currencies of value: *love, joy, peace, and happiness*. Giving and receiving are one, the same. In order for you to have or receive, you must give it. If you want anything, say love, you have to have it in yourself, and then you must give it freely. The flow by its own nature will return to you.

As mentioned earlier, God is giving and receiving unto itself. It makes sense because God is all in all. The identity behind every mask is Him. When you give to others, you give to yourself. When you give to yourself, you give to others. When you love yourself, you love God. When you love God, you love yourself. When you help others, you help yourself. When you help yourself, you help others. This is God flow.

The world truly is a mirror and not a metaphor. When you look into a physical mirror with your spiritual eyes, you see exactly who you are: *God*. When you look into a physical mirror with your physical eyes, you see how you are expressing yourself as who you think you are or as you know you are: *either God or not God*. By this I mean, if you appear youthful, healthy, and joyful, then God is flowing through you more, whether you are conscious or not conscious of it; if you appear aged, unhealthy, and unjoyful, then God is not flowing through you as readily. You are eternal so you do not "age" as you have been misinformed. The vitality in you diminishes because the flow is retarded and so you appear "aged". The dynamic flow of God is working and reflecting its state back to you always.

The world is a mirror of the human collective too. The state of the world reflects if God is flowing well within the individuals that make up the collective as a whole. War, poverty, and dis-ease demonstrate He is not. God is actually always present and waiting for his prodigal son to return but the prodigal son is unconscious of this until he actually returns home where there is love, peace, and harmony.

CHAPTER 15
Love

♦

You hear it often said, "God is love God loves you." What does this really mean? What is this love thing?

Love is an ambiguous word with a great deal of baggage.

Just to confuse the issue more, the scriptures separate love into different categories. There's *phileo* love which refers to the love of friendship; there's *storge* which refers to the love of family; there's *eros* which refers to sexual love; and finally there's *agape* love which is the divine love.

Love is commonly perceived in our society as merely an emotion. We say things such as we "love chocolate," we "love a good party," we "love our spouse," and on it goes – but we are referring to the emotion of feeling what we term love. These forms are but mere physical expressions of a deeper spiritual love. You are unable yet to conceive of a love devoid of or unattached to some personal interest.

Recall earlier I said that words belong to the world of form; that they cannot truly express that which has no form; and that they ultimately create separation. As soon as something is named or labelled, it creates separation. When I say, "I love you," "I love God," "I love chocolate," I have separated the two objects here by the word love. The usage unintentionally obscures the connectedness between them and between love itself, the oneness of all. Without a diligent conscious recognition of this, God and love becomes separated and gets lost to the point where it eventually does not exist.

I can hear you utter, "Say what?" What I've just said may sound senseless, confusing, or pure blather at the moment. In essence, love is not separate from you.

Love and all its relatives (ie. joy, peace, happiness, et cetera) are natural states of your being. What does this mean?

Let us look at God, our Father, who you've heard loves you unconditionally.

As established, you are a divine being. What gives you your divine essence is that you have the freedom to embrace and experience whatever thoughts you desire. And that divine essence, called free will, is love. In the scheme of nature, we are a privileged species in that we have been given free will. It is the gift of love from God to each of us. Each of us has the divine essence of will so that we have the freedom to create uniquely whatever ideal we envision through thought.

However you choose to use your free will, whether for "good" or "evil", the Father will never judge, condemn, or persecute you. To the Father, all things are pure in their state of being. You can do with thought whatever you will, for the Father's love for you is steadfast.

The love between you and God has no condition. God loves you in complete freedom to do as you will, for your will is His will. That is the covenant between God and His sons, God and Himself. Whatever you do, wherever you venture unto Him, you are always loved.

Love in its ultimate form is the desire of the Father to allow the life that He is to be an ongoingness through each of you. The purest form of love is the freedom of will that the Father gave each of you so that through the exercise of that will, you would explore the dimensions of thought and expand yourself into a greaterness, which expands the mind of God.

Recall earlier that I mentioned there are parallels here. You may have heard of the term 'tiger parents'. One possible aspect of a tiger parent is they impose their ego and free will on their children. They dismiss their children's own desires and push them to become lawyers and doctors instead of artists and carpenters, because the unGodly society persuades them this traditionally makes more money in this survival game it falsely created. They live vicariously through their children to compensate for their own failures. They justify their actions as love because it is in the best interest of their children in this unGodly world.

The true parent who unconditionally loves their child is as God is and does as God does. She wants nothing more than her child to be happy; to do whatever brings them joy; and to be whoever they wish to be. They allow their children the freedom of their own will.

This demonstration of love extends to all relationships: *family, friends, and strangers.* You do not exert your will on others just as you wish no one exerts theirs on yours. You do not have any desire or expectations of others to be this or that. You do not judge, criticize, or condemn others based on what you think is right.

God is all in all. God is absolute, whole, and complete. You and God are one. You do not need another to make you whole and complete. You already are. You are one with yourself. When you are not, your thinking of love is misguided.

When you exceedingly desire and need the boy or girl, it generally indicates you are incomplete. The relationship will not complete you as you think for that within yourself is not. Though you claim you love her, you may have expectations of her. Consequently, you judge her when she falls short of them. This may result in frustration, resentment, and possibly infidelity. You continue to think that when love fails you, it's because of the other person.

This unGodly world has glamorized and defined love for you. Movies often portray love as stemming only from a physical attraction. Love at first sight quickly moves to 'getting jiggy with it' and then happily ever after. Those unconscious quickly accept this as love and mimic what they see constantly depicted in movies. You can see today that many relationships fail. Marriages and families are broken. Many are confused about love.

As said, this world is backward. All is spiritual. The physical is spiritual manifest. When you know who you are and are spiritually aligned with yourself and God, you lay the foundation for a relationship. When two individuals who do not know who they are form a relationship, they will find themselves having to "work" at it.

When you are complete within yourself, you do not long for that special someone. It does not mean that you do not desire one but you are non-attached to the outcome. You are still joyful and at peace with yourself.

Contemplate how great the love of God is, that He allows you to be and to create for yourself anything you wish, yet never judges you. God loves you in complete freedom to do as you will whether it is good or not-so-good. Contemplate the love that He has for you, such that He manifests for you every thought you embrace and every word you utter. Contemplate it.

The best and surest way you may know God is love is when Selfless Love fills your heart. There is a strong compelling urge to help someone, to heal their ills, to relieve their suffering, to bring them happiness, or to point them to the Truth. This is perfect love.

No matter how vile or wretched you perceive the life of your brothers, who themselves are divine beings exercising their own free will, to God, they are still pure and loved. You are a divine being. You are a child of God, made of this same core essence of our Father: *love*. So to be the love you are, you articulate the same love that the Father has for you as when you were created. You express it to yourself and to all others. God is within you. You are the same. You must do the same.

Love presently may seem far-reaching and elusive because you have not completely assimilated who you are. Until you completely assimilate who you are thereby becoming the absolute state of love, make love a choice. Make love a habit. That is, you intellectually and consciously choose to be a loving person toward all. When you do this continuously such that it becomes your being no longer doing, when you become and remain conscious of the truth of who you are, your divinity radiates automatically.

Love is the spiritual blood that circulates your divine being. Love is the stream of consciousness that flows through all of life and you are like a sieve of this ever-moving river of which you receive and encapsulate. Love is the cosmic glue that holds everything together.

Love is not something you do. Love is what you are when you are just being. Love is the true nature of your being. Love is who you are. Do you now see that love is not separate from you?

CHAPTER 16
Joy

♦

If you pause to observe, you will notice a certain joy a flower somehow exudes just standing in the soil; a certain joy a dog generally exudes when roaming a park; a certain joy a happy baby naturally exudes doing nothing. At the same time, if you pause to observe yourself, you will notice you reciprocate a similar joy from the mere observation of all the examples abovementioned.

In all cases – the flower, the dog, and the baby – each radiate the natural harmony of the universe. Your inner spirit is filled with joy from the purity of these other beings. They have not given you money to profit from; they have not baked you a cake to enjoy; they have not given you their time to help you accomplish something; they have done nothing for you and asked nothing from you. Yet you are in joy. This is because they unconsciously remind you of who you are and what you are ironically searching to achieve or restore.

The flower, dog, and baby do not busy themselves with doing something in order to become something. They do not see themselves separate from life and so want nothing of themselves. They are one with what life wants, which is nothing but to be. They do not judge themselves whether they are beautiful or not. They do not ask or demand of another to tell it that it is beautiful. They sense, no matter how obscurely, their rootedness is in Being, the formless and eternal oneness of life: *God.*

You are as the flower. You enter the world with a unique perspective and set of talents, which enable you to blossom an aspect of natural intelligence that has never been expressed before.

This mad world ruled by the UnGod has intentionally prevented you from knowing who you are and obscured you from the joy of your natural being. This mad world has you constantly busy in the doing of something – making you feel that you are productive; that you are accomplishing something; that you are good because of your sheer busyness. You have become less concerned about simply being the soul that you are – making you feel that part is insignificant.

I know that when someone's Being is closer to who they are, then everything else falls into place; everything they do is generally good for it all stems from their Being. Conversely, when someone's Being is farther from who they are, then everything else is inconsistent; generally not everything they do is good for it stems from their Being. I can observe and confirm it easily through the tiniest of their actions from such things as the way they treat others, the way they perform their work or any task, and the way they respect nature.

You are here to be joyful as you define joy, not as society or another does. When you think, act, and feel joyful, then you are in the natural state of your being: *God*, for that is what He is. When you stay true to your inner self and your desires, you will always be aligned with joy.

Joy is true freedom. Joy is the freedom to express yourself without judgment from yourself or the world. Joy is the freedom of being without fear, guilt, or shame. Joy is the freedom to move about wherever you please. Joy is the knowing that you are creating life on your own terms.

Joy is the grandest state of being. When you are in joy, you cannot be in negative states like fear, envy, anger, greed, insecurity, guilt, remorse, lack, or conflict. When you are in joy, you have no time to hate, hurt, or besiege anyone. When you are in joy, you are at peace with everything about you. When you are in joy, you see God in all things. When you are in joy, life is a wonderful adventure you hunger more of. When you are in joy, you are inspired to do great things. When you are in joy, you are in God flow.

"How do I become joyful?" I can hear you ask. By knowing who you are and that you are eternal and infinite. Because then you know that every moment of your life gives you the freedom and opportunity to express joy by creating life on your own terms. No matter the madness you see in the world around you, there is nothing that is ever worth separating yourself from happiness, joy, and God – *nothing*. Love yourself completely through and through for you love God when you do.

Daryl Chang

You are a creator here to live only as your soul urges you to do. Know that you always have the option to change your expression at any moment you desire. You are here to add to the beauty of God's landscape. You have the power and freedom to rightly do what you want to do and become who you want to become. When you have done this, by your societal conditioning, you will attach a meaning that it was your "destiny".

You must go beyond societal conditioning that you must do this or that, or that your destiny is this or that. You must get down to the business of being, living explicitly in the moment. You will find a grander happiness and a greater freedom than you have ever known before. You will understand what it means to be your authentic self. Your purpose is to be. When you focus on being the joy you are, the doing is an afterthought that happens naturally on its own.

CHAPTER 17
Silence

♦

I have a mantel clock that sits on my desk. As you might already know, any analog clock makes a ticking sound. Even if I put my ear to my watch, I will hear it. However, through the din of the surroundings, like noise from the furnace, the window outside, and the radio, I don't ever hear the clock ticking. There is no ticking sound even when the room is technically quiet. That is, the furnace has paused momentarily, the outside is serene, and the radio is off. Even my fidgeting, moving around, and not being still makes the ticking sound inaudible.

One day, I decided to intentionally meditate. It was only then when I was in my yogi position, sitting completely still and remaining silent, that I heard the low but unmistakable tick-tock.

I describe this instance to illustrate that the world you live in now is similar. There is nonstop noise such that you cannot hear the still small voice of God until you sit still in silence. God is spirit and He speaks in a silent inaudible voice that you can only hear with your spiritual ears. Silence means you arrive at a place of complete stillness. This place has no thought; no chatter from your false self; no physical movement; complete emptiness of everything; just space. This space is for God.

God is actually speaking to you constantly. He speaks to you through human physical appearances, emotions, passions, and desires; and through the voice of experience and human knowledge. His most intimate conversations though are through the still small voice. You need to be still to hear it. There, He lovingly takes your hand, guides, and protects you as you would with your own child.

Haul every thought out of the home of your mind. Clear the entire space and give God carte-blanche to fill it as He pleases. He is an amazing designer and will do an amazing job redesigning your home.

Daryl Chang

While everyone else busies themselves with all of the things they do in their days, learn to be quiet, and still and solitary. In stillness lies your connection to the mind of God that can orchestrate an infinity of details for you. The turbulence of your internal dialogue and that of the external world and social consciousness is allowed to become quiet. You will get in touch with the innermost essence of your being.

To reach a state of no-thought means to reach a state of higher intelligence. The Higher Intelligence, God, is able then to work automatically without interference from your limited human mind, one that is presently filled with utter nonsense. A spiritual discipline is required only. All others – mental, emotional, and physical – will fall into place.

No-thought provides that space or gap from thought that self-proliferates. Creating a definitive and adequate "space" provides a stillness between everything. Space is a pause, a gap, a psychological distance that can provide perspective, peace, stillness, comfort, relaxation, reflection, introspection, calmness, a slowing down, a chance to breathe, recovery, restoration, contentment, a glimpse of joy and happiness.

In order for you to get acquainted with God, your True Self, you must learn to be still, to quiet your human mind and body and its activities so that you are no longer conscious of them. To commence, I recommend you sit quietly in a relaxed position. Focus on your breath as you inhale and exhale. Breath is life. You cannot breathe of yourself. God lives in you and breathes through your lungs. What you feel is His Presence. Get acquainted with this feeling and embrace it so that you feel His Presence in your daily life despite not being in a sitting meditation. This is true meditation.

When you are at total ease, speak these words slowly, imperatively, and quietly to yourself. "Be *still!* – and KNOW – *I AM* – GOD." Take in the significance of these words. Without thinking, allow this command to penetrate every cell of your body, every part of your mind, and the deepness of your soul.

This command though seemingly simple is very significant. All is consciousness down to the cell of your body. The command to be *still* is issued to not only the whole of your person as you perceive but to all the cells of your entire being – I recommend picturing your cells during the first trials; to not run off with Lil-i thoughts; to not be misled by your false self; and to not physically move.

The command to *KNOW* is to remind you that this is not an exercise of faith, hope, or belief. It is an established fact.

The latter part of *I AM – GOD* is to remind you of who is the One saying this. Though you are saying it to yourself, be conscious that it is God speaking not you per se. You and your entire being are obeying His command. You and God are One, so technically yes, you are saying it to your self, your True Self.

During the initial times of this practice, I can suggest you add the words, "within you". That is, "Be *still!* – and KNOW – *I AM* – GOD – within you." It may help you to easier receive these words for yourself. You are conscious of the I AM consciousness that is commanding the forces of your mind, emotions, and physical senses to be still. Know that You – *the God of you* – speaks and must be obeyed. Eventually, after persistent effort, you will realize that you are that Consciousness, and that these forces are listening to and obeying you. You become the true master of your self. To say it in another manner – after some time, you may feel it unnecessary for you to say the extra words "within you" for you will no longer think yourself separate from God anymore. You will be confident and know that when you say I AM, it is because YOU ARE.

When you learn something, you cannot unlearn it. The exercise outlined above may possibly take immediate effect. You may straight away begin to live this truth. On the other hand, this may not necessarily be so. Accordingly, you must persist in this exercise until you reprogram every cell of your entire Being. It requires diligent practice.

It is akin to obesity. An obese person does not become obese overnight. He gradually attains this state over time, and either didn't notice or chose not to notice his unhealthy condition. When he does decide he wants to make a change and lose weight, he must recognize that it may not be an immediate process as he wishes. He can start an exercise regimen, say walking fifteen minutes a day. After one week, he may feel he has not made substantial progress in losing any weight and that it does not work. But this is not so. Progress is being made and with more time and discipline, he will eventually bear fruit.

This may similarly be the case with this routine. You have become obese with dead weight from the ego's management. When you recite the suggested words, it may feel like nothing is happening. There may not be any dramatic changes in your body where trumpets start playing. But if you persist in your efforts with time and discipline, you will notice one day that you are much lighter than when you started out.

It is not adequate to intellectually know that God is within you. You must know it in the depths of your soul. When you submit to it, you will then know I AM, *God*. Say it often, a thousand times if you have to until it seeps into your soul; until it reverberates through every cell of your whole body; until it assimilates into your entire being.

I was going through the ritual of saying these words mechanically when one day God and life suddenly hit me with a two by four. At long last, it dawned on me that I won the lottery. I hit the jackpot. I won a million gold pieces of love, wisdom, and power. I was rich. I was jumping up and down in joy like a banshee inside. I was in total jubilation. All is consciousness down to the cells of my body. When these words, said in its completeness, are fully absorbed by every cell of your being, the energy force will transduce any malfunctioning cell back to its perfect God state. How great is this?

I make time to go into silence often nowadays. I say these words to myself. In actuality, God is the one saying it to me. I'm just obeying His words and recognizing now that the "I" (Big-I) is Him, not the "i" (Lil-i) that I thought I was before. I allow Him to speak, guide, and inspire me with fresh thoughts and ideas. Throughout the day when I'm in midst of activity, I am conscious to take the practice of silence with me. It is doable to still align yourself and make connection with God even when not in a ritual position.

Your life, from the time you were born and came out of your mother's womb, has been like the 100 metre dash at the Olympics. The gun went off and you bursted out of the starting position. You have been competing, running fast as you can on this track. The roar of the crowds has drowned out the Master Coach who has been by your side all along. If it wasn't for the noise, you'd hear His sage advice as you walked, not ran this path. You would have stayed in your lane and not be disqualified for obstructing another. You would have optimized your time to the border line which is God Country. You would have received your gold medal of love, joy, and peace.

Instead of hearing the thundering crowd screaming, "Run! Run! Keep running!" you would have heard an initial calm voice say, *"Be still and know I am God."* As you continued down the path, you would have heard the voice continue, *"I am your Shepherd. You shall not be in want. I will make you lie down in green pastures. I will lead you beside quiet waters. I will restore your soul. I will guide you in the paths of righteousness for My name's sake. Even though you walk through the valley of the shadow of death, you will fear no evil for I am with you. My rod and My staff will comfort you. I prepare a table before you in the presence of your enemies. I anoint your head with oil. Your cup overflows. Goodness and love will follow you all the days of your life. You will dwell in My home forever."*

CHAPTER 18
Thought

♦

God the Spirit is the invisible formless unmanifest. God the Man is the visible form manifest.

Thought is God in its most exalted form. Everything that is has come forth first from thought, which is the supreme intelligence called the mind of God.

To think with your heart <u>and</u> mind is to create.

God is within you. You need only to recognize you are one with the very Power that created you. You need only to accept your power. You need only to think the thoughts as God intended and as God does.

At present time, many have been distracted from the spiritual realm and fixated on the physical realm only. This is because the UnGod is clever and wants you to not even think of the true Spirit God. Remember, all is spiritual. The physical is spiritual manifest.

When you have a thought-form, your present habit is to go seek and take material from the forms of nature, and make an image of the form which is in your mind. For instance, when I wanted to make a coffee table, I went to get the physical wood, glue, screws, et cetera. You have so far, made little or no effort to co-operate with Formless Intelligence; to work "with the Father": *God*. With your limited human mind and lack of consciousness, you have not dreamed that you can do what God does.

You reshape and modify existing forms by manual labour. You have given no attention to the question whether you may not produce things from Formless Substance by communicating your thoughts to it. In actuality, you may and can do so. You need to understand and accept a few fundamental propositions.

There is a thinking substance from which all things are made, and which in its original state, permeates, penetrates, and fills the spaces and interspaces of the universe. A thought, in this substance, produces the thing that is imaged by the thought. You can form things in your thought, and by impressing your thought upon this formless substance, can cause the thing you think about to be created.

You are created in the image and likeness of God Himself. You are a creator and thought is the spiritual clay with which you sculpt your heart's desires.

Until you progress to absolute knowing, always add and reinforce your thought with steadfast faith and belief. Hold your thought until you feel and embrace the joy and happiness from its fulfillment. Remember, everything you need and desire is already fulfilled.

Divine thoughts will surely externalize themselves in a divine life. Thoughts of power will end in a life of power. Great thoughts will manifest in a great personality.

Do you understand now why you hear the phrases such as, "I think therefore am," "Be careful what you wish for," "You are your thoughts," "If you think you can or think you can't, you're right," and "What you think you become."?

Remember, all is spiritual. The physical is spiritual manifest. When you think of something, it means it exists in consciousness and is real. It lives. Your thoughts are real. When your thought process is proper, there is an unspecified but definite time for its physical manifestation.

The thought principle is sound. Though I have included this chapter, I feel that there is a caveat regarding its practicality. Thought is not an insignificant or trivial matter. It is quite on the contrary. I think it wise and worthy to pause and reflect on this for a moment.

Your mind is both a transmitter and a receiver. Remember too that we are all One Mind. Your Big-I receives and your Lil-i transmits or thinks. Big-I is your True Self with the Divine Mind of unlimited intelligence. Lil-i is the false self with the human mind of limited intelligence. It is necessary that you learn how to think and how to know Your thoughts.

Daryl Chang

God is within you. He has made you in His image and likeness and given you the power of thinking to create. What you think or believe, you are. Your body, your personality, your character, your environment, and your world are what they appear to you because you have thought them into your present status.

If you are conscious of God, then you will think with the mind of God and think rightly – the true things you wish to think. You will experience all things good.

If you are unconscious of God, then you will misthink or think erringly. If you allow your false self, Lil-i, to be the master of your thinking, then you will have unGodly thoughts. You will experience things like conflict, poverty, and ill-health.

You are of your own free will however you appropriately decide to use thought. Your actions are your self-responsibility. If you use thought currency for your own selfish gain, then you are the one who must accept responsibility for its consequences. Undesirable negative consequences that result are there to make you weary and to teach you so that you eventually learn to turn back to Him.

I recognize I have the power to create through thinking. However, as mentioned in the last chapter, I go into silence for the sole purpose of attaining a state of no-thought so as to allow Him to speak to me; to allow Him to provide my thoughts which are His. I recognize now that I am simply a vehicle through which He expresses Himself.

The Higher Power and Higher Intelligence that grows the grass, the flowers, the trees, the animals, and all mankind is the same Higher Power and Higher Intelligence that grows me. He develops the grass, the flowers, the trees, the animals, and all mankind to the maturity of their expression. And so it is with me. He develops me to the destiny of my expression if I open up to allow Him.

I like to often remind myself of this with relatable ideas so that I don't slip back into my limited thinking. That is, He is the Driver and I AM His passenger along for the ride. He is the Director of the film and I AM His actor for the role He wants me to play. He is the Jockey and I AM His horse He reins. He is the Recipe Maker and I AM the baker who follows His recipe. He is the Sun and I AM the sunbeam. He is the Electricity and I AM the wire that He flows through. He is the

Shepherd and I AM His sheep. He is the Vine and I AM a branch. He is the Gardener and I AM the branch He decides to cut if I do not bear Him fruit.

I correspondingly recognize now that I am a focal point of God's Consciousness and Intelligence. I can do nothing on my own contrary to what I thought in the past. I AM, *God within me*, is doing the work. Through His guidance, I merely follow His direction and observe the resultant experiences. I entertain possible troubles if I slip back into thinking with my limited human mind. I have no real desires of any kind because I know I have everything for which He has already provided. As such, I try best to limit my Lil-i thinking. When I can consciously at will enter into complete communion with the I AM, *God of me*, then all is well. I am humbled. Life is simpler and better this way.

CHAPTER 19
I AM

♦

Though knowing the truth of who I AM was a moment of grandeur for me, I admit that it did not spontaneously erase the existing state of being or unGodly habits. However, I got this far so I just had to keep going. It was simply a beginning to a renewed life. God Country was a new place I moved to and planned to set my roots here for the rest of my Earthly life. It was exciting to start assimilating into this new culture.

So now I know God is within me. I am one with God. This is to say, with humility, "I am God." In the beginning, it felt funny to say it. But then with full realization and acceptance, I'd say it wholeheartedly, enthusiastically, and repeatedly. Obviously, I do not go around saying this out loud to anyone. Nor do I go around loudly asking others, "Do you know you are God?" Most would think I was mad. The big unGods though would arrest me, lock me up, pump me up with loads of psychotic drugs, and throw away the key because they know it's true and don't want anyone getting right ideas from me to form a collective mass and overthrow them. This truth is unintelligible in an unGodly society.

The statement, "I am God" is never made as an audible statement. It is uttered in the silence of your own soul. The only way it is ever voiced is in the natural radiation of authority, perfection, and power that emanates from this inner secret acknowledgement. It isn't that difficult to do actually. You cannot do this by means of blind faith but that is unnecessary. You accept it as fact. I get over my Lil-i self and move on detached. It is the same way when I say, "I am Daryl," "I am hungry," or "I am writing this book." It is simply an acceptance, a certainty, and a knowing. It is what it is.

I found it helps when I can reaffirm it in other ways. For example, God is the Superconscious, so it's appropriate to view His physical manifestation as Superman. When I see the portrayals of Superman, he knows he's Superman and that bullets don't harm him, so he's fearless against them. I know that I am God so I am invulnerable to the bullets of the unGods.

For the most part, I've always thought well of myself. I am self-confident, self-assured, and self-worthy. I never really thought too much of what I did or how I did things. Though I was not conscious of such, I did things naturally right, evident by my general surroundings and life. But along the way, I had a personal traumatic experience and thereafter things were not occurring rightly or smoothly for me anymore. When things aren't going "right" and the way you "want" them to, you start to think to the point of overthinking. You start to think about what it is you are doing "wrong" and how to go about "fixing" it.

It's like when I watch a clearly talented athlete who consistently shows his brilliance but one day he has a bad game. Somehow, he gets thrown off. He lets the one bad performance get to him. All of a sudden, that instance sets off a spiral of bad games uncharacteristic of the athlete. He starts to think of how to fix his game. He's gotten off the track of simply being and naturally doing from the time when he wasn't thinking much. That is how it was for me.

I, like I'm sure many others have, tried much of the ubiquitous self-help advice, particularly positive affirmations. It was odd because somehow before I had a quiet confidence I didn't need to verbalize. And here I was doing these positive affirmations. I'd say things like, "I am beautiful. I am charming. I am funny," and I did believe in what I was saying to myself because it was true to me but it didn't seem to have a dramatic effect overall.

This unGodly world had conditioned me to view things as good or bad. I didn't realize it but I started making effort to not be "bad" as I thought it to be. I'll give you an example. In general, being humble is considered good and being arrogant is considered bad. So when I was saying positive affirmations, I didn't want to be arrogant so I felt a bit pretentious to some degree for saying it. Isn't that silly?

As said earlier, there is nothing good or bad, only the thinking makes it so. So to think and say arrogance is bad is a false statement. Arrogance is a part of you as is humility. If you're being chastised at the store by a rude employee for something small, for which she is possibly wrong about, arrogance can serve you. You do not tuck your tail between your legs and take the abuse. You stand your ground and assert yourself firmly. So in such a case, it isn't "bad".

Pride is another example that can work that way too. You take pride in how you dress nicely so you put on a shirt and jacket instead of a t-shirt and gym pants to a party. You take pride in everything, which you think is a good thing. But then you're wrong about something and you take pride in never being wrong or at least you don't want others to know you were. You don't admit your mistake honestly because of your pride. It doesn't serve you. In this case, it's not "good".

When I discovered that God was within me, this daftness ended. With this realization, I knew that whatever positive affirmation or compliment I paid myself, it was absolutely true. It's similar to how easier it is to give someone a compliment than it is to receive one in this unGodly society. Someone compliments you, "You're beautiful," and you bashfully dismiss it, "Aw shucks, no I'm not."

So when I now say to myself, "I am beautiful, I am charming, I am funny," I say it with conviction and I receive it with confidence because I AM.

It makes sense that I should naturally feel this way because God is within me. I am an extension, an expression of Him. When I say I AM this or I AM that, it is beyond blind faith or belief. It is the acceptance of truth. I recognize the I AM speaking is my True Self; that It is speaking to my human self. Have you heard that these are the two most powerful words? Do you know where it's coming from? Do you now see why that is? You say it and you claim it. It's that simple.

God is within me. I am one with God. I am a part of Him. I am a cell of His Body. I am an attribute of His Mind. I am a faculty of His Intellect and Intelligence. Recognize this is true for you as well.

I'd like to share a springboard list you can begin to practice on. It's not necessary but just for fun, you may want to gaze at your eyes in the mirror as you initially recite them. Now that you've assimilated to some degree the information in this book, be mindful of who the "I" is saying it and see if you notice anything. Say them boldly. Say them often.

I AM GOD. • I AM SOVEREIGN. • I AM FREE.
• I AM ETERNAL. • I AM DIVINE. • I AM LIFE. •
I AM WHOLE. • I AM POWER. • I AM LOVE.
• I AM UNLIMITED. • I AM LIGHT. • I AM JOY. •
I AM PEACE. • I AM WISDOM. • I AM HAPPINESS.
• I AM BEAUTY. • I AM ABUNDANCE. • I AM HEALTH. •
I AM ALL-KNOWING. • I AM WORTHY. • I AM GREAT.
• I AM LOVABLE. • I AM ATTRACTIVE. •
I AM IRRESISTIBLE. • I AM SEXY. • I AM LOVED.
• I AM ADVANCING. • I AM WONDERFUL. •
I AM BRAVE. • I AM.

I know that I am one with God when I feel peace. I feel peace because I am no longer erroneously thinking in my limited capacity that I cannot do this or that. Now in my unlimited thinking, I have trust in God to let Him do the work. I am able to assert a positive idea and act upon it with trust and complete mental realization. If I am apprehensive, anxious, or fearful, then I know I am depending on my own strength – *the false self*. I have slipped back unnecessarily into the conditioning of this unGodly world. I catch myself and remind myself that I have His strength to lean upon.

The more I assimilate who I am, words like hope, try, seek, believe, have faith, and forgive have lesser to no meaning. These are only of the limited human mind. They all indicate doubt, uncertainty, and lack of love. God is all-knowing. The main thing I have is gratitude for He has provided everything to me and to us all.

Not everyone tills gently the soil like the farmer does. Not everyone moves gracefully like the ballerina does. Not everyone paints fluidly like the artist does. Not everyone thinks the way I think about things. Not everyone organizes their thoughts the way I do. Not everyone is willing to take the time to write a book like I do. God put something inside me like He did the farmer, ballerina, and artist. He put something inside you too. If I don't do these things, I don't rightly honour Him. If I don't do these things, I fail Him. I fail myself. I write this to affirm I understand the nature of my existence so that you subsequently can affirm yourself the same. It is me allowing God to express Himself through me. This is why I AM here.

There is a Higher Power at work. The workings of this universe are choreographed with elegant precision and unfaltering intelligence.

There are no accidents, coincidences, or chance encounters. The limited human mind will dispute this but you and I must be conscious of this always.

In my limited human mind, I entertain thoughts such as, "Maybe I am supposed to write this book. Maybe others are meant to read it. Maybe the book helps restore God Country. Maybe this. Maybe that." If I do not honour myself and God, for certain, I will not get to see, understand, appreciate, and experience the truth of this possibility. So instead, I do; I write the book.

This is why I have to be non-judgmental, non-attached, and non-resistant. I do not judge anything because I don't know. I do not get attached to an outcome I think I want. I don't know. I do not resist the process. I don't know. God is all-knowing so if I think with my limited human mind instead, I hinder the possibility of things. But God is within me and I am one with God, so actually I am all-knowing too. So with my unlimited God mind, I do write this book for others to read and help restore God Country. I am always at the right place at the right time. I am always where I am supposed to be, doing what I am supposed to be doing. That is my desire and intention so I shall express and fulfill it. I know this. This is why I AM here.

Are you driven internally by God to do what He tells you to do to uniquely express your self? Or are you driven externally by this unGodly society to do what it tells you to do to commonly survive?

CHAPTER 20
The Ultimate unGod

♦

The Ultimate unGod is the one deemed the opposite of God. For the sake of brevity, I refer to the Ultimate unGod as UnGod – with a capital U – hereon. He has several well-known names by which he is referred to. I intentionally do not write them here or anywhere throughout this book. As mentioned, deemed opposites are illusions. I do not acknowledge him. He does not exist in my consciousness. There is only God. Hence, for illustrative purposes, I describe him as the UnGod, the ultimate in the continuum of what God is not – *the Ultimate Dark Ego.*

The UnGod is the cleverest of all the unGods. He is the pioneer and leader of the unGodly world. He has his big unGods – *the big dark egos, the top doGs* – working at the highest level for him. Like God, he is unseen. Unlike God, he has no true power. He can only have power through the illusion of power. This illusion of power is harnessed and gained through the unconsciousness of God's lost children and is sustained by the contrivance of fear. He '*has blinded the masses of those who don't believe in God, so that they are unable to see the glorious light of the good news shining upon them*'. He does not hide anymore in the shadows and yet many in this world cannot see him still.

Please do not take offense to my next statement. Unbeknownst to you, you are working for the UnGod. You are not on his payroll though because you volunteered to toil for him through your own free will. "How so?" I can hear you ask.

The UnGod has built an exceptional army of soldiers to serve him and keep him on the throne of his fabricated kingdom. He is your adversary who '*goes around like a roaring lion looking for anyone to attack*' and devour. He tenaciously recruits new soldiers every second. He recruits his soldiers illegitimately through their silence of implied consent. He is very subtle in his scheming ways.

The UnGod is very clever in how he enlists you as his soldier. God is within you. You are naturally a good person. You are born this way. You are loving, joyful, and generous.

You decide one day you'd like to renovate your kitchen. You do your research and finally settle on a contractor. Unsuspectingly, the UnGod sends one of his soldiers disguised as one. A cordial exchange is made. He agrees to start Monday but says he requires a $1,000 deposit. You give him the money and he leaves. You don't see him ever again and realize you've been swindled. You become angry. The joy you had envisioning your new kitchen is gone. You are now distrustful, stingy, and less loving not just to another future contractor but with all persons in general. Bam! You have been recruited by the UnGod and working for him free. You are now a traveling ambassador, salesman, and marketer for the UnGod. The unGodly contractor did his job and will continue earning his keep. You have begun your new trade alongside your other societal roles.

The aforementioned is just an example of how the UnGod recruits you subtly. The fact is, because you were born into this unGodly society, you have been bathed in many instances of recruitment. The recurring instances have cumulatively reinforced his training and groomed you to be the soldier you are today.

The UnGod's legion continues to grow. All who lack consciousness and don't know who they are contribute to the development and sustenance of the UnGod's false kingdom.

Those who alert you to the UnGod and spread the message that God is within are demonized, mocked, or discredited immediately and greatly in this world. This truth is unintelligible in an unGodly society. Jesus carried the same message during His time and was stoned for blasphemy. The same is still going on today.

Are you offended when you read or hear this message that God is within you? "Yes," I think I hear you say faintly. You are offended or in disbelief because your ego and proud human personality cannot and will not accept this idea for that would mean you have been duped. You feel your intelligence is insulted. The ego's life is severely threatened if this truth takes a firm hold of you. It knows then it cannot live, thrive, and dominate your thinking, your emotions, and your actions of old. This is the ego's modus operandi. This is its ploy – to make you always doubt the existence of God within you, your True Self. The true Master would succeed the rightful position should you ever accept this truth.

This is why the UnGod has such a strong foothold in this current world. Many souls whose ego has been their Master for an inordinate time now will not embrace this truth and venture to investigate its veracity. Their identity would be lost. They would need to accept self-responsibility for their own lives and lose their luxury of blaming others.

If you truly reflect, you will notice that the more you shirk your self-responsibility, the more your burdens become.

As mentioned, the definition of crazy is doing the same thing over and over and expecting a different result. I trust it is evident that all these dark egos, the big unGods, who set themselves up as authorities under false illegitimate governments are only liars, deceivers, manipulators, tyrants, and false masters. If you truly have had enough of war, poverty, dis-ease, et cetera, recognize that they are not natural conditions. Changes must always be made first in you, the individual. You must stop delegating your authority and proclaim it yourself. Your habit of attributing powers to others in false illegitimate governments and denying them to yourself is what keeps you forever a slave. If you remain unconscious, do not claim your divinity, and exercise your power, for certain, an unGod will jump at the opportunity to exercise his over yours. The power is not in the external world. It is within you.

You who witness the atrocities of this world such as war, poverty, and dis-ease may have unceasingly wondered why this is so. Note, *'we are not fighting flesh-and-blood enemies but against evil rulers and authorities of the unseen world'*. The evil ruler and authority who is unseen is the false self, the ego. The evil rulers and authorities are the dark egos who control the lesser egos of the unconscious souls and who demonstrate their false authority in this false world. Armageddon appears to be a battle without (ie. physically outside) but it is battle that must first occur within. It is the battle between God and unGod within. An apocalypse appears to be happening without but it must first happen within. It is God crushing the unGod within. A crucifixion as exemplified by Jesus appears to occur without but it must first occur within. The ego or human personality must be crucified within so that you may rise in consciousness to Oneness with God.

Daryl Chang

The UnGod seems to have a totalitarian and insurmountable hold that seems not easily broken but that is an illusion. Each individual here and there who awakens to the truth of God; the truth of who they are; and the truth of the One Mind shall shift us back to God Consciousness – the perfect state. You are one such individual.

CHAPTER 21
The UnGod and
his False Kingdom

◆

There is a legend about a famous Zen master, an elder named Hakuin. He was sought by many people for inspiring teachings. One day, a samurai warrior came to visit him. The samurai said to the master, "I want to know heaven and hell. Do they really exist?" The old man replied, "Who are you?" to which the samurai replied, "I am a samurai." The master retorted, "Ha! What makes you think you can understand such deep subjects? You are merely a callous, brutish soldier. Go away and do not waste my time with your foolish questions!" The samurai angrily exclaimed, "How dare you insult me! I'll kill you!" Hakuin remained calm and said, "You see? This is hell." The soldier was taken aback. Humbled by the wisdom of Hakuin, he sheathed his sword and bowed before the Zen master, who then gently said, "And this is heaven." We create our own heaven or hell. We create God's Kingdom or a false one of the UnGod.

You are presently living in a false world; a fabricated kingdom of the UnGod – *the proverbial hell.*

Remember, God is the only one who has true power. The ultimate ego, the Ultimate unGod, has no true power. He is a false authority in this world. He has to create the illusion of power by taking the power from the relatively lesser egos of unconscious souls, those functioning with the limited human mind.

God the Unlimited Mind, the All-Knowing has One law that is eternal and immutable. It is universal, exists and applies to anywhere in the universe regardless of location. He expresses as love, knowledge and wisdom, peace, prosperity, sovereignty, freedom, togetherness, and order.

In contrast, the UnGod, the ultimate limited mind, has formed man's laws of which there are many and are continually escalating. His laws are not universal. They differ with location based upon the whims of unGodly legislators. They are not eternal and immutable but forever changing based upon the whims of unGodly legislators. He expresses as fear, ignorance, greed, confusion, control, and chaos. He contrives fear, the food or energy source of the ego, to sustain his false kingdom.

Recall earlier I defined illusion as that which changes. Unlike God who is eternal and immutable, your life is constantly changing moment to moment; hence your life is an illusion. An illusion is based on and created by your unGodly thoughts. This man-made world formed by collective limited minds creates man-made laws that are forever changing. These unGodly laws are intentional to persistently limit love, knowledge, freedom, and oneness. The UnGod is a monster with an insatiable appetite for its food source of fear – the energy source that sustains his existence. Hence, you see dominant expressions such as hatred, anger, greed, envy, selfishness, stress, confusion, worry, and anxiety resulting in the never-ending atrocities of war, destruction, death, poverty, dis-ease, et cetera.

The definition of crazy as you know is doing the same thing over and over again expecting a different result. Many seem everlastingly oblivious that not much has changed over the years. There is still war, poverty, dis-ease, et cetera so it should be very evident to you that we are doing the same thing over and over again; that the big unGods representing themselves as governments are cunningly creating the illusion that they are working and fighting to rectify and better things; that governments are false illegitimate authorities who serve their own interests; and that you are being used as pawns and puppets in their sick, demented game.

"What am I supposed to do?" I think I hear you say.

It is paramount that you begin to know you who are. When you do not, you are easily intimidated, manipulated, and enslaved by the UnGod's tactics. If you do not, the big unGods will have you do things that are immoral, incorrect, and harms others – things you will deny.

For ages throughout history, the UnGod's big egos, the big unGods, have gotten you to follow their false illegitimate orders because you lack consciousness and intelligence. They have hypnotized you such that you equate being good as obeying their orders. You absolve yourself of self-responsibility. An individual's personal responsibility to choose correct over incorrect action for themselves is always their own. You can only erroneously believe and claim that you are "abdicating" personal responsibility for such choice to someone else. It can never actually be done in reality. The responsibility always belongs to you. You do not think for yourself. You alone have allowed your intellect and humanness to betray you.

Here are some examples of your blind obedience.

- You blindly obey orders to assail blacks because the big UnGods – *false authorities and culprits* – told you they are animals.
- You blindly obey orders to kill other races because the big UnGods – *false authorities and culprits* – told you they are not your kind and are evil.
- You blindly obey orders to constrain women because the big UnGods – *false authorities and culprits* – told you they are inferior.
- You blindly obey orders to harass and enforce citizens wear masks because the big UnGods – *false authorities and culprits* – told you they are selfish and the cause of dis-ease.
- You blindly obey orders to inject poisons into yourself and others because the big UnGods – *false authorities and culprits* – told you that you are protecting yourself and others.
- You blindly obey orders to arrest innocent people because the big UnGods – *false authorities and culprits* – told you they are guilty.
- You blindly obey orders to assault peaceful protesters because the big UnGods – *false authorities and culprits* – told you they are criminals posing as such.
- You blindly obey orders to restrict family members from visiting their loved ones in long term care facilities because the big UnGods – *false authorities and culprits* – told you that you are protecting elders from dis-ease.
- You blindly obey orders to poison the air, the food, and the water because the big UnGods – *false authorities and culprits* – told you that you are doing your job properly for the betterment of society.

- You blindly obey orders to snitch on a neighbour because the big UnGods – *false authorities and culprits* – told you he is breaking a law created by them (illegitimately).

Blindly following orders should never be seen as a virtue by anyone who considers themselves a moral human being. Genocide is the result of following orders. A person who knows who they are would not blindly follow orders from a false authority. They are their own authority.

Remember the ego has no identity of its own so it seeks one, particularly one that gives them a semblance of power. When you identify with a societal role, you confuse the perception of yourself – *your true self*. Likewise, you confuse the ego you perceive in others as their identity. It is the work of your own ego that uses its misinterpretation to strengthen itself through being right and therefore superior, and through reacting with condemnation, indignation, and often anger against the perceived enemy. This strengthens the sense of separation between yourself and the other, whose "otherness" has become magnified to such an extent that you can no longer feel your common humanity, nor the rootedness in the One life that you share with each human being, your common divinity.

You can observe the unGodly nature of persons playing their societal role in all interactions everyday everywhere. A woman playing a cashier acts indignantly toward a customer role who does not obey her order to wear a mask, an order from ignorant false authorities. She has lost her humanness, loving the power she's assumed from her role. The man playing a policeman acts haughtily toward a driver role who did not "stop" at a stop sign. There was no harm done but he has lost his humanness, loving the power he has assumed from his role and issues a ticket fine because of an illegitimate man-made law. A woman playing a teacher heavily scolds a student role who does not obey her rule to raise a hand to ask a question. She has lost her humanness, loving the power she's assumed from her role. The UnGod and his big unGods have trained its citizen pawns well for the roles they play.

As I've established, what you give to others, you give to yourself. What you give to yourself, you give to others. Anyone who is conscious and of right and sound mind, would not deliberately harm themselves or make themselves suffer. To demonstrate and emphasize consciousness and unconsciousness, let me pose a few questions. Which of the following would you intentionally choose? Peace or anger/conflict? Happiness or unhappiness? Joy or sorrow? Love or fear? Fun or no fun? Smiles or frowns? Most people would choose the former option of the given choices. Those who choose the latter may believe that they are consciously choosing so, but this intentional suffering is misguided and a reflection of unconsciousness. Why do you not always react the way you know feels better and automatically choose so that you escape unwanted suffering?

The big unGods are harming others, for certain, and thus harming themselves. They bear the seed of their own eventual destruction. Some souls are apparently lost but the big unGods are in the desert, the middle of nowhere. They are the bullies that overcompensate for their weaknesses; cowards who pretend to be strong and unafraid. They have lived so long in hatred and fear of their fellow human beings, that they have greatly developed their faculty of hatred and fear. That is all they know and who they have become. They have separated themselves completely from their brothers and sisters. Their souls have totally forgotten God within. You who are unconscious are relatively the same albeit of a lesser degree at present moment. The big unGods are the epitome of unconscious souls ruled by their ego.

Though they are unconscious of it, the big unGods are the most insecure and fearful souls projecting this aspect of themselves outwardly. They find solace in other unconscious souls who also deeply fear. The big unGods need a gargantuan teddy bear hug. Darkness cannot be dispelled with more darkness but light. Fear cannot be dissolved with more fear but love. I send love and light to the UnGod, his big unGods, and the little unGods to fill their void. May God open up their consciousness.

Ignorance and tolerance are two great sins you commit that help sustain the UnGod's fabricated world. When you are ignorant of who you are and when you tolerate the intolerable things such as war and destruction, you contribute to the false kingdom you detest.

You judge and condemn the tyrants, dictators, murderers, child molesters, pedophiles, human traffickers, et cetera evil. You judge and condemn the atrocities of war, massacres, genocide, planet destruction, et cetera evil. You believe the unseen dark entities who you give names deemed opposite to God are evil. When you are unconscious, you know not that you are part of this evil you abhor; that you partake and contribute indirectly to this evil you loathe.

Know who you are. The unGod of you is partaking in the evil of this world. When you see this and accept self-responsibility, you will take the steps needed to no longer be a part of this false world. Recognize that each soul who discovers and lives the truth of who they are, contributes to the collapse of the UnGod and his false kingdom.

God is within you. He is a part of you as you are a part of Him. The unGod is also within you; he is also a part of you as you are a part of him. The two exist as parts of you to allow you to discern what is not you so that you can know what is you. Once you know both, then you know One, and then you know to know only One: *God*.

You, the God within, will not be intimidated, manipulated, and enslaved by the UnGod.

All is spiritual. The physical is spiritual manifest. Resolving the problems you see in this unGodly world by busying yourself through physical means is not the most effective approach. You are being attacked spiritually. Begin with yourself first. When each person knows and lives the truth of who they are, this unGodly world will collapse. The Kingdom of God/Love/Heaven will be restored.

CHAPTER 22
The big unGods

♦

You probably already know the famous Bible story about Adam and Eve. The story goes that God Country originally existed in its pure form but it started to fall when the first man sinned. That is, he disobeyed the word of God. The story of Adam and Eve demonstrated how it began. Eve was deceived by the unGodly and clever serpent to eat the fruit from the Tree of Knowledge that allowed for the first illusion of judgment. Adam followed Eve by doing the same when she offered him the fruit. They suddenly perceived they were naked, and then upon hearing God's voice, hid in shame because they knew they had disobeyed God. But God being God saw them no matter how well they thought they hid. When asked, Adam shunning responsibility for his own actions, blamed Eve for his disobedience.

The same has continued to this present day. Many clamour, complain, and whine of the tyrants, dictators, murderers, war, poverty, violence, greed, anger, hatred, and other atrocities in the world. They blame others and also God for these undesirable states but in their own lack of consciousness and self-responsibility, perpetuate the crimes. They look always outside of themselves to conveniently blame others, while beneath they hide in shame because at some level, they know they are guilty of the sin as well.

If you know who you are, you would not commit sin. If everyone knows who they are, they would not commit sin. There would not be any sense of need for a false authority to police sin. You are already the authority. There would be no relevance for it.

If the majority know who they are, while a few remain unconscious, there would not be a semblance of a false authority developing because the majority know to police themselves. The few unchecked egos would still try to usurp its master but conveniently conform because that is what they do.

I have often wondered, "How did we get here? Really, how did we get here?"

Ages ago, it seems that the number of people believing in God outnumbered the people who didn't. In both cases however, the factions generally did not and still do not understand God.

When I look back in history, men of unGodly nature formed religions to intentionally control people and nations. They created images of God and dogma for the purpose of intimidating the masses into a controllable organization. The dark egos of religion were very clever for it did not have to govern and rule people through the sword. They only had to perpetuate the teaching that God was not within their reach, that all knowingness and all power was not within them. They used fear as a tool to keep them in line.

Many have been deceived that God is outside of them and accepted it as a truth even to this day. I observe that sincere ones of no mal-intent are teaching the word of God, blindly repeating the original teachings of these dark egos, unknowing of its falsity. They sustain the unGodly work that has taken a strong foothold.

Remember, egos are not God. They are the unGod. They have no identity of their own so they seek one, particularly one that is God-like. They have no power. Hence, they have to give the illusion they have power. Their power exists only when others give theirs to them. They have no kingdom so they have to fabricate their own false one.

Your unconsciousness of who you are allows them to freely do everything aforesaid. You voluntarily pay homage to the Ultimate unGod. The UnGod has his cleverest disciples at the very top: *the big unGods*. These big unGods rule the subordinate unGods in this world.

The big unGods are very clever. They have distorted the image of God. They have misled, confused, manipulated, intimidated, deceived, and enslaved all. Many know not that the true God is good; that God is within not without; and that the true God has been replaced by a false UnGod. They have implemented endless propaganda to this date so that many no longer suspect their deception and elaborate schemes; that many don't know God is right under their noses.

The big unGods have successfully defamed God to create numerous factions. They have fashioned atheists to not believe in God; agnostics to not know what to believe of God; and firm believers to believe in God outside of themselves and a God of their making. They have mixed lies with truths to create confusion and misunderstanding of God. They have shaped copious religions across the globe to compete and fight amongst themselves as to whose God is the true God. They have manipulated all to be pawns to unconsciously serve the Ultimate unGod in his fabricated and false kingdom.

I know individuals who apparently have had dreadful experiences brought up in religious families. They are now completely turned off by the mere mention of the word God. They view God with absolute disdain. This is unfortunate because they prevent any discussion of the true God; because they will not presently turn to Him; and because they impede their own soul advancement. As mentioned, much of church and religion are established to manipulate minds for their own agenda.

The big unGods are very clever. From the beginning of time when the first man sinned, they have endlessly preyed upon your unconsciousness. They have deceived, misled, and trained you to look for God outside of yourself always and never to look inside of yourself; to look only at the physical realm and never at the spiritual realm; to look at your neighbour with fear and never with love; and to look to them for guidance and never to God or yourself.

The big unGods are very clever. Everything they do is to eradicate God from you. Everything they do is to detach you from your spirituality and your consciousness. Everything they do is to have you make them your master, your false god. Everything they do is to separate you from every fellow human being, every creature, every thing of nature – the sun, the air, the water, the lands, et cetera. Everything they do is to separate you from God.

They cage, abuse, and mass kill animals for pleasurable consumption beyond satiation. They exploit animals for testing in the name of human safety. They confine animals into unnatural environments in the likes of zoos, aquariums, and safaris in the charade of science and entertainment. No other creature does such things to other creatures.

They destroy forests and lands of nature's habitat to other creatures in the pretence of food systems and economic growth. They pollute the air in pretence of fumigating germs that they've made you believe make you sick. They contaminate the lands and water with chemicals, pesticides, and synthetic fertilizers in pretence of human safety.

They have cunningly manipulated your mind to separate yourself from animals and all of nature. You were then susceptible to separate yourself from your fellow human being. They desensitized you. They made you readjust a new normal of the temperature in the soon-to-be boiling pot. Just as they had done with the animals, they extended it to humans so you did not notice. There is prevalent human and sex trafficking, particularly of the most vulnerable, children.

To continue the separation, they craftily create countries, religions, and factions of all sorts to divide and conquer. They make you turn on yourselves. You participate in the conquering of yourself and others.

The big unGods are very clever. They have formed a clandestine alliance. They have tactfully set up a worldwide survival system of countries, banks, money, corporations, governments, churches, organizations, institutions, libraries, medicine, entertainment, law, property, media, and schools in society. They have infiltrated and commandeered the entire system, set themselves into positions of false authority, and direct the slaves of the system. The entire system is fraudulent and rigged for their benefit. This alliance is the epitome of the Mafia. Notwithstanding, the saving grace is that in the system, there are souls with checked egos through which God still flows.

Even the little mafias and tyrants within society know not that they are unconscious slaves to this alliance. As explained earlier about unchecked egos, they are unconscious of themselves and unconscious of the part they play in the scheme. Those unconscious, whether you deem them "good" or "bad", do not know that they are mere pawns and puppets in this orchestrated system. You have "good" people doing "bad" things to anyone and everyone because they lack consciousness to act morally or right, even in spite of knowing it is so. Such persons simply carry out orders because they have been hypnotized and trained by the system to equate obeying authority as "good". This happens at your ordinary shop where staff members follow illegitimate orders from false governments, reprimanding customers who do not obey. This happens at military operations where soldiers assault peaceful protesters. They are doing the dirty work for those higher above. They have unsuspectingly become the gestapo blindly executing false illegitimate orders. On a grander and extreme scale, you have genocide.

The big unGods are very clever. They are constantly training you to be evermore lazy, self-irresponsible, and dependent on others. That is, to willingly be professional slaves. They seduce you with conveniences like driverless cars, touchless payments, and delivery services of all kinds. They cunningly eliminate physical contact of any kind to train you to eliminate spiritual contact too.

The big unGods are very clever. They created a system based on survival. They created money for the workings of this system. You have never questioned the basis for it or the false authority behind it. You have never questioned how the false authority is so privileged with the ability to print money as they deem while you cannot. This is understandable because each generation simply accepts the reality handed them by the prior generation, assuming this is life and in their best interest. You have become an economic slave. Hence, you will never have true freedom. You are forever their slave.

Every creature on this Earth in his native state has economic freedom. Man is the only economic slave on Earth. They have deceived you to be such by your unnatural wants and acquired desires. They perpetually seduce you with images of glamorous lifestyles of actors, celebrities, and athletes. You fantasize and strive for the same. When you are unable to, you judge them to have more skills, gifts, and talent than you and that you are incapable of greatness yourself. Your unconsciousness is the ball and chain that binds you, who are the slaves of want and desire.

You have bought into this game of survival based on money, a mere piece of paper. It has been perverted so much as to have unyielding power. You are enthralled by its power. You fight against another robustly so that you can have more than the other. You can never have enough of it. You beckon to its call automatically and yet you are not any happier for it. You have been told a lie that the world is running out of everything. They have distorted abundance into scarcity and you have bought into it.

Money is quicksand. The more you get sucked into its vortex, the more anxious, the more hurried, the more stressed, and the more depressed you become. Their economic system has engendered you with selfishness and greed rather than generosity. You may be capable and competent to do anything but you excuse yourself from your capability and competency to do it because there is no money in it; because nobody will "pay" you for it. Many times you have the intention of creating something "good" but it never happens because you get stopped in your tracks by "Where am I going to get the money?"

Now that you have made money your master, they have conveniently created banks and financial institutions to control money. You have given them the key to your control as their eternal economic slave. They implement worthless programs with labels like RRSP, TFSA, and high-interest savings accounts under the sham of maximizing your money to keep you tied to their system. They have falsely self-proclaimed authority and capability to seize your money if you are a disobedient slave. They have created an unsuspecting army of soldiers under the guise of employee roles. Tellers, financial advisors, bank managers, and police officers are the gestapo who blindly obey orders to control their fellow human beings who play the customer roles.

They created and seduced you with convenient digital systems such as credit cards, debit cards, and loyalty cards that allow them to track your money behaviour. If you were to spend cash person-to-person, they cannot trace you otherwise.

Thomas Paine stated, "Man did not make the earth, and though he had a natural right to occupy it, he had no right to locate as his property in perpetuity any part of it; neither did the Creator of the earth open a land-office, from whence the first title-deeds should issue."

If it is true that "What I make is mine," then anything that existed independent of human effort belongs to no one. I am a thief if I take something you made without your permission. So, to claim ownership of such a thing such as the land, the rivers, the animals, the trees, the air, the water, or the sunshine, would be tantamount to theft and the epitome of it.

At what point did God's realm become someone's realm, into the realm of "mine"?

There is no legitimate ownership of so many things on this earth because they do not exist through anyone's labour. Someone stole it and it happened by force and manipulation without any regard but for themselves.

This is robbery. And the unGodly system we live in blindly or otherwise is perpetuating the crime. Laws were made and continually are, by men, thieves themselves to legitimize their ill-gotten gains.

We have gradually twisted things in this unGodly world to suit our perceptions, to transform a right to a benefit into outright ownership. God created everything in such a way that all things be possessed in common. "Nature is the mother of common right, usurpation of private right." It and its fruit are common to all, rich or poor.

After centuries of world and human regression, even a squirrel has more wealth and freedom than you or me, to do what it wants, when it wants, wherever it wants, and however it wants. Indigenous people and every living thing had the run of the land, air, and water. They had the simple freedom to say, "Let us climb that mountain. Let us swim that lake." No one has such freedom today. And now even the squirrel has to rudely contend with a human saying, "Get off my land you pesky thing, you have no right to be here."

I am a thief. You are a thief. We are all thieves. The UnGod and his big unGods have made us unsuspecting and guilty accomplices in their pilfering. The reign of the UnGod must end. It begins with each one of us to recognize that we are God's children; that we inherited His kingdom; that He granted stewardship of His kingdom; and that we have been negligent in our responsibility.

God has given us all everything but the UnGod's economic system has deviously made everything a commodity, even our own natural being. Everything is monetized and has a price, otherwise it cannot be obtained. Life is a consumer item.

If after reading the above you have not come to a personal realization *still*, I will boldly tell you now that you are working for the UnGod and his big unGods.

The big unGods are very clever. They establish institutions throughout the entire elaborate system to have their slaves work inside and outside of it. They create mercenaries inside to be their gestapo executing their filthy work for them. The inside slaves think themselves as employees

Daryl Chang

doing their job for themselves ignorant they are doing a job for the Mafia. The outside slaves think themselves as independent persons who are served by the inside slaves. All inside egos play a societal role enjoying its societal power to exert on other egos playing a subservient societal role. You can observe this interaction in every setting of the big unGods' society.

At a hospital, doctor and nurse roles serve the patient roles. At a police station, officer roles serve citizen roles. At churches, pastor roles serve patron roles. At government offices, tax collector roles serve taxpayer roles. At the retail store, cashier and sales associate roles serve customer roles. At banks, teller and financial advisor roles serve money collector roles. At law offices, lawyer roles serve law abiding citizen roles. At courts, judge roles serve criminal roles. At schools, teacher roles serve student roles. The inside soldiers are slaves themselves within their own institutions once they are finished with their shift for the day and become the counterpart role they had just served. Though your human personality is "good", your unconscious soul has been deceived to sustain and propagate the institutions of the UnGod's system. The big unGods have ingeniously built a monstrous self-propelling machine.

The big unGods are very clever. They created a system and much technology to track and monitor you, their slaves, of your whereabouts and in everything that you do; for without knowledge of you, you cannot be a slave for them. They created churches where you voluntarily register your marriages. They created hospitals where you voluntarily register birth certificates for your children, giving them ownership of your children. Each unsuspecting parent perpetuates the system for their manipulation. They created tax and revenue offices to track and monitor the status of their slaves. They entice you with scraps of illusions under the facade of child and spousal benefits.

They created DNA services under the sham of helping you determine your ancestry. You have been preyed upon and seduced by your curiosity. You have freely given them your DNA thereby reducing their time and effort to locate you should you ever be a disobedient slave; to eradicate your race should they deem you unneeded anymore; to harm you with target specificity.

From the time you came into the world, they have used you as pawns and puppets in their deceitful game. You have enslaved yourself and helped them enslave your fellow human beings. You have allowed them to give their illegitimate orders for which you blindly execute, keep yourself and others enslaved, and harm others to some degree.

The big unGods are very clever. They do not want you mentally and physically stimulating yourself from spiritually within. They seduce you with mental and physical stimulation outside of yourself. They do this with movies, sports, music, video games, social media antics, and reality shows. You are continuously looking outside yourself at others, comparing yourself, and thinking you are incapable of more.

The big unGods are very clever. They want to keep the unconscious soul focused on the outer physical realm never to ponder and seek the inner spiritual realm. They create physical disasters and atrocities. They seduce you with all things that can appeal to your physical desires and pleasures like smoking, drinking, and watching porn. They bombard the entire landscape with images of bountiful hedonism.

The big unGods are very clever. All that they do is for the purpose of incessantly increasing separation – *separation from God and your neighbours*. They inundate you with ideas, images, and illusions of good versus evil: *portrayals of superheroes and villains, police and criminals, democracy and communism*. They inundate you with steady propaganda of dualities or polarities by cunningly providing illusions of choice: *liberals or conservatives, medicine or sickness, education or manual labour*. They flood you with the unvarying message that you must compete and fight and that one must win (at all costs) and another lose: *sports (individuals and teams), manager position or regular staff, reality shows about survival of the fittest*. They do this to keep you in judgmental and critical mode, and to generate hatred for self and others.

The big unGods are very clever. They intentionally create a relentless noisy and distracting environment so that you cannot hear the silent voice of God. There is never-ending noise produced from television, music, traffic, sirens, horns, debates, disasters, war, and global conflicts. The noise and distractions keep your mind full, cluttered, and unthinking.

The big unGods are very clever. They keep you overwhelmed, busy, stressed, confused, and engender fear and anxiety to keep you in survival mode, and make you feel exhausted and defeated. They ensure this by making society run 24/7. There is no day of rest. There is

Daryl Chang

continuous television and media – hypnotic devices – to spread their propaganda. There are work shifts round the clock. There are systems within systems to work through. There are piles and piles of paperwork and useless details with every task or service. They created a legal system with its own language so that it is complex, incomprehensible, and perplexing to navigate. They intermingle lies with true facts to create confusion and doubt so that the baby is thrown out with the bathwater.

The big unGods are very clever. They ensure that your physical and mental well-being is always compromised without your knowing. They wreak havoc on your entire body. They discreetly poison the air, food, and water with chemicals and invasive frequencies. When you are sick from their making, they secretly poison you more with their bogus science, unnatural medicine or concoctions, and hypothetical advanced treatments. They create fake establishments to give you the illusions they are fighting for cures. When you are in pain, you cannot think properly.

The big unGods are very clever. In present day, they enforce lockdowns and social distancing to ceaselessly increase separation. They endeavour to retard any encounters between an unconscious soul and a conscious soul thereby reducing the possibility of any awakening. They enforce face masks so that persons are faceless to eradicate warmth, visual display of positive emotions, and general humanness.

They have trained you very well to keep your distance from your fellow human being even before this manoeuvre. They have trained you to ensure you keep yourself separate from another; to lose your divinity and humanness. They have trained you to not willingly give or receive help from a random soul.

When a person is coming toward me as I walk, I will look at their eyes to acknowledge them. More often than not, the individual will look down, look away, or stare into the distance beyond me. Sometimes when I am walking around the neighbourhood after a huge snowstorm, I will see an elderly, a woman, or someone who is exasperatingly shovelling the snow bank formed by the city plough. I will stop to ask, "Are you okay? Would you like some help?" Their answer has always been "No." I can see it in their eyes that they are suspicious of my motives; they decline because they do not want to feel indebted thinking that they must repay in kind; they think it is a ploy for money.

This reminds me of a joke you might have heard already. The joke goes such that a great flood had come over a land. The waters rose so high that it forced a man to climb onto his rooftop. A man in a rowboat came and offered him help. He replied, "No thanks, God will save me." Some time later when the water was at the man's waist, a fellow in a large motorboat passed by and offered him help. He again replied, "No thanks, God will save me." The water continued to rise higher and higher. A helicopter suddenly appeared above him. The pilot announced over the loudspeaker that he would drop a rope to help him get on. The man on the roof replied, "No thanks, God will save me." The waters rose to greater heights, and alas, the man drowned. When the man arrived in Heaven, he rushed over to God and said, "Heavenly Father, I had faith in you to save me and yet you did not come. Why?" God replied, "I sent you two boats and a helicopter. What more did you expect?"

God wears many masks. Because you don't know who you are, you are unable to see God in other fellow human beings as well. God is all in all. Everything is working with elegant precision and unfaltering intelligence. He is always available and sending you help, particularly when you explicitly ask for it. The help arrives in various forms.

Yes, the big unGods are very clever. They do all these things so that you look to them as god your saviour and to never look within. The unconscious soul has been forever hypnotized. They ensure that you do not have time to contemplate God, life, and who you are. They've conditioned you well to distrust those who tell you that God is within.

They will not stop till you are wholly removed from God. Consequently and conveniently, they can intimidate, manipulate, and enslave you along with the unconscious masses for their selfish motives. They do so with the illusion of power when really they have none. They have power only because you and other unconscious souls who do not know who you are, give away yours.

I'm always amazed at the influence of the big unGods. The physical appearances of the big unGods are very unhealthy and unsightly aged; the tones and mannerisms are fake, untrustworthy, and suspicious; the track records have repeatedly shown them to be liars, cheaters, and fraudsters; yet so many souls in this unGodly world swiftly accept, obey, and fulfil the counsel and orders of the big unGods on health, economics, and spiritual matters. I suppose each needs the experience for their evolution.

The UnGod and his big unGods have trained you well to keep yourself separate from every human being, every creature, and every thing of nature – the sun, the air, the water, the lands, et cetera.

So the charade goes on. But the Law of One, the Law of God is just, immutable, and beneficent. If you renew your mind and transform yourself, your world and that around you change to reflect your new consciousness. You do not need to apply for a visa, book a ticket, board a plane, and fly to God Country. All is spiritual. Time, distance, and space are illusions. Once you know truth and live truth, you are there. The physical is spiritual manifest. That is how it is. You need not concern yourself with others and you need not look to others outside yourself but your own.

I trust it is easy for you to see now that one big doG can lead other lesser doGs with them. Lesser doGs conform to another because that is how they are. The pack follows their false leader.

That's why if God is the Master, the Shepherd, He leads His sheep (the doGs) to God Country. If the sheep (the doGs) are lost, they follow a wrong and false shepherd that leads them away from God Country.

If you have a good shepherd: *God*, and if you have good sheep, then you have a good life and a good home: *Heaven/God Country*.

If you don't have a good shepherd: *UnGod*, and if you don't have good sheep, then you don't have a good life and a good home: *hell/the current world*.

If you want a good life and a good home: *Heaven/God Country*, then you need to be a good sheep and follow a good shepherd: *God*.

You, who are unconscious, are not fighting flesh-and-blood enemies but UnGod rulers and authorities of the unseen world (ie. the *doG* that is within you, as well as the *doG* of others outside of you).

CHAPTER 23
The Extinction of the UnGod, the big unGods, and the unGods

♦

It always amazes me when people use words like impossible, incurable, and improbable. When I hear this, I say quietly in my mind to them, "So you don't know then. Nothing's impossible. You just don't know."

Here's a funny dialogue. It'll go something like this. Some person will say to me, "There's always going to be war. It's human nature. I'd like peace but I'm just one guy. It's impossible." I'll remark, "It is possible. You realize when you say that, you're part of the problem. We won't have peace because you don't think it's possible. If you multiply you by a billion people who think the same, it makes it less possible. We are all One Mind, so if you instead believe it is possible, then it makes it more possible." Of course, without truly knowing who they are, my comment doesn't make a dent in their erroneous thinking.

When you know who you are, everything is possible.

At one time, in my limited thinking, war and violence did not make sense. Once I knew the truth of who I was, I started to make sense of it. Beneath your humanness, you are God, an eternal and infinite Being. An infinite being has no beginning and no end. It is eternally expanding by its own nature. If another tries to restrict your expansion, or put another way, restrict or take away your freedom in any capacity, you will automatically resist because it is unnatural to you.

Recall earlier I mentioned that because the nature of God is eternal and infinite, He cannot be contained. Any attempts to restrict His expansion will fail. Also, God is perfect good. God is wholly love, joy, peace, and all things good. God is persistent in maintaining His perfect good state.

If God strays from the perfect good state, He will always automatically correct Himself to reinstate His perfect good condition. This is reflected in the physical world as we see today.

The UnGod's contrivances of fear and all its negative cousins resulting in war, poverty, dis-ease, et cetera shift God away from His perfect good state. But God is always working to correct Himself, so those souls who still possess love will counter the efforts of the UnGod. Within all of God's creations is the seed of good because that is who He is. Thus, they have the capability to correct themselves. All souls are God's children, seeds of His Greatness. If a soul does not become conscious to correct himself, then he will destroy himself because that is not his inherent nature. I like to view this as an ingenious safety mechanism that God put in place so that He continues His expansion. God destroys out of man's nature, that part of Himself, which operates against life.

When a soul, who is point of consciousness, destroys himself, the physical body disintegrates, the cell separates, and the expression of his work is completed for its time. But God is eternal. So the physical form may no longer exist but the spiritual point of consciousness will reappear in another form at a later time. You can observe this easily in nature. Leaves fall off a tree, decompose itself into the earth to provide valuable nutrients to the surrounding life, and reappear in another form we humans know not.

God, the Higher Intelligence and All-Knowing, is always operating to correct Himself. The unconscious human, who knows not who he is and thinks with his limited mind, cannot and will not be able to see or know this. He does not see God at work. Instead, he sees only the physical atrocities of fear and he self-proliferates them.

Anyone who is trying to manipulate, intimidate, and enslave you is unGodly. They are unconscious of who they are because if they are, they would know that it is senseless and unnecessary. Because you don't know who you are either, you buy into this game of deceit. As a result, you give in to your human tendency to fight and rationalize that it is self-defense; and that it is necessary. It sounds reasonable but fundamentally, hatred is hatred is hatred and killing is killing is killing, no matter the reasons behind it. So the madness continues on and on.

"So how do you propose I stop?" I can hear you ask. Disengage from the UnGod, the big unGods, and all unGods. When you engage with an unGod, you are acknowledging its existence. When you engage with an unGod in any like capacity, such as fighting, arguing, or disputing with him, you are sustaining his existence because you provide an opponent. Without you, he has no power.

Let's say you are playing the board game 'Monopoly'. If a player lies, cheats, and keeps changing the rules to benefit themselves only, especially the banker, would you keep playing? Does it make sense to keep playing? I think I hear you say, "No." If you keep playing, then you will never win the game. You will only have false illusions of victories. You know the game is rigged now. You're not enjoying the game anymore as when you thought all were equal. You know it's just a game. You'd rather play with others who aren't liars and cheaters. There is no point to playing the game anymore. Is this any different than this unGodly world rigged by the big unGods where they have you playing their game?

Know your truth. Live your truth. Create not compete. You create and live a new truth instead of contributing to sustain another's. Disengagement will not be instantaneous. We are all mired in this unGodly world for so long that it seems intimidating to even try. You still have to "survive". You're in this system and you want to get out of the system but you don't know how. However, don't blindly trade this unGodly system with another that appears godly. If others are still unconscious of who they are, then the new system still has potential to progress into just another unGodly one. The same egos still exist but in an apparent new setting.

All is spiritual. The physical is spiritual manifest. First, spiritually disengage from the unGods of this world, including yours, in its entirety. It's better to do it fully at once but if you need to, little step by little step is still good. It's like tearing off a band-aid. If you're able to extricate physical aspects too, then that is a windfall. The complete physical disengagement is of an unknown timeline. But it is certain.

The unGods will have no one to oppose them or feed them. When enough Gods know and live their truths, the unGods will cease to exist. The unGods will have become extinct. When the unGods cease to exist, things such as greed, hatred, and envy will cease to exist. God Country will be restored. Heaven will be a place on Earth.

Unable to envision a new world, a child grows up accustomed to accepting whatever reality is handed her.

When you have been in the habit of doing something for a very long time, you sometimes don't realize how locked in you are to it. It seems unthinkable to be doing that something in a different manner, even if it's in a better manner. Your limited mind keeps you there because your doG likes familiarity. He's comfortable. He likes routine. Your doG likes his doG days. He's content with his conditions even it's less than desirable. He tolerates it. Even if it'll make his life better, being lazy and not doing anything feels more pleasurable at the moment.

I mentioned earlier, that in God Country, money has no relevance and does not exist.

Can you imagine a world where you can't wait to get up in the morning? A world where as soon as you awaken, you are immediately in joy and enthusiasm. You don't get up to "make a living". Instead you get up and do those things that you do to add beauty to the landscape of God Country. You don't worry about having money, food, shelter, et cetera because everything is provided and available to you so that you can do what you love to do. Can you imagine that? I do. I want you to sincerely imagine it and hold it in your heart.

"Sounds nice but it's impossible," I can hear you say – *my heart is crushed a little*. Tradition is a fancy word for being lazy. That is, not to grow and do things better if possible and if you really want to. You must not just know the truth, you must live the truth.

I'd like to walk you through a sample scenario of promising individual interactions between God and a few unGods.

> unGod 1: Wait, you want us to work our butts off and then provide electricity for free?

> God: Yes.

> unGod 1: We need money so we can buy food. How are we going to feed our families?

God:	I will get the guys who grow the food to give it to you free. If they do, can you give the electricity for free then?
unGod 1:	Yes.
God:	Thanks.
unGod 2:	Wait, you want us to work our butts off and then provide food for free?
God:	Yes.
unGod 2:	We need money so we can buy food. How are we going to feed our families?
God:	That's a silly question. You grow food. You can already feed your families.
unGod 2:	You're right. But we need money to pay the electrical guys so we can run the irrigation pumps to water the fields.
God:	No need. I spoke to the electrical guys. They'll give the electricity free if you give them the food free. Can you?
unGod 2:	Yes.
God:	Great. I'm gonna to speak to more guys.

If you take unGod 1 (electrical) as a point of consciousness, join it to unGod 2 (agricultural), another point of consciousness, you have started a line of consciousness. If you take another point of consciousness and join it to unGod 2 (agricultural), you now have a bigger line. You keep adding more points of consciousness as required until you ultimately join unGod 1 (electrical), the first point of consciousness. You have now formed a closed circle of consciousness. By this time, the unGods have willingly participated to act more Godly. The unGods were unfamiliar and not conscious of the final result to be. Now expand the circle of consciousness. You now have a perfect sphere of consciousness – *One Mind*.

Daryl Chang

Every thing is an entity. An individual is an entity. A present corporation is an entity but it consists of individual entities. If each individual unGod comes to understand who they are and is cultured with the larger picture, then a collective entity would share the vision. If the entire financial world got behind the God principle, it would be the greatest influence to restoring God Country to the point where it eventually discontinued its existence. There is no reason that God Country cannot be formed if the frogs desire to jump out of the existing unGodly pot to begin the process.

Now, restoring God Country may possibly seem like a daunting task to you. Do not be overwhelmed. Do not be anxious about the future. Do not be overly concerned what others are thinking or doing. Just be willing to learn, understand, and accept who you are. God will lead. The sheep will follow.

If you have fully comprehended the teachings in this book and not slipped back into your limited human mind, you will appreciate that it is not impossible a task. God is within you. You are a vehicle for God. Your duty is simply to know "what" you want. God's role is the "how, when, and where". God is always working with elegant precision and unfaltering intelligence. All is spiritual. The physical is spiritual manifest. Recall that any desire you have means that it is fulfilled. The manifestation is real. If your desire for God Country is in your consciousness as it is in mine, then it is in Universal Consciousness. The seed of that desire is born and needs time to fully blossom. Think not that it is not so. We are all One Mind. If each person takes self-responsibility, comes to understand who they are, and desires the same, then God Country shall be.

Through my own free will, so be it.

CHAPTER 24
Desire

♦

Desire is a funny thing. Desire can be a tricky thing.

God is everything. I am one with God. So, I have everything. He has provided everything for me to have and use. As such, I recognize that I do not have any real desires because they are all fulfilled.

God is eternal and infinite. He has a perpetual desire to expand. I am simply a vehicle for His expression to expand Himself. He instils a desire within me to guide me in the direction of the expression He wants of Himself.

God has given me a superpower – the ability to create and manifest my desires through the thought of my Lil-i, the thinker of me. God is perfect good and all-knowing. If I follow Big-I's directions through the words God speaks silently to me, then I experience all things good only. I experience an abundant life for this is His expression through me.

On the other hand, my ego and human personality thinks he is separate from God. He doesn't know he has been given everything. As such, if I think with my limited human mind, Lil-i, I earnestly desire things. My doG likes to roam and explore so he desires a lot of things.

If I am unconscious that the Big-I is the true Master, then Lil-i marches to the beat of his own drum and toots his own horn. Lil-i uses the superpower not recognizing that the manifestation of things is possible only through God's power, not his. I can use the superpower to manifest any desire I want for personal enjoyment. God has no issue with this. He wants me, His child, to enjoy life's beauty because if I enjoy life, He enjoys life. The world is my oyster. He gave me everything to have and use.

However, Lil-i is able to use the superpower indiscriminately. He can use it for selfish gain at the expense of others. This would be unGodly.

Though Lil-i acquires his desires, he will have to possibly deal with not-so-good (ie. negative) consequences. God does not judge me for this; He forever loves me. In such cases, these are lessons that are to teach and have me turn back to Him. It is a longer scenic road.

The Big-I is wise. The Lil-i is clever.

I have the knowledge to create a knife. Lil-i, being clever, can use the knife to harm someone. Big-I, being wise, will use the knife to cut food and make a delicious meal. I have the knowledge to manifest anything I desire through thought. Lil-i, being clever, will use it personally for physical pleasure with no higher purpose but self-interest. Big-I, being wise, will use it impersonally for God to express something unique that adds to the beauty of mankind and God Country.

This is the difference between cleverness and wisdom. Knowledge is the accumulation of facts. Knowledge can be used for "good" or "bad". Cleverness is creativity acting on knowledge. Cleverness can produce a knife and cleverness with selfish intent can use it to harm someone; cleverness can use it personally for physical pleasure only. Wisdom tells you what to do with the knowledge. Wisdom is the ability to discern what matters and does not matter to find true purpose. Wisdom takes the same knife and cuts food to make a delicious meal; wisdom can use it impersonally for God and a higher purpose. Wisdom is fundamentally more important than knowledge and cleverness.

You will observe many personalities in mainstream media of this unGodly world spewing the law of attraction and how to use it to attain what you want. Remember, human personalities are of the ego. They are focused on the physical world and the physical pleasures they can get from it. They are devoid of any spiritual higher purpose. They have knowledge of the principle, tool, or mechanism and they are clever to use it for self-interest. They achieve "success" as defined and measured in this unGodly world. They are proud of their knowledge and seduce you to live as they do. They do not teach or inspire you to go beyond for they know not.

I observe multiple replicas of celebrity personalities in religion or spiritual societies spewing the word of God; preaching about God as a third person outside of you; telling you how to be and act in order to receive favour from Him and to receive the desires in your life. Again, these are human personalities who apparently do not truly know themselves either.

If you recall in the description of Oneness, this principle also applies to the intellect of the limited human mind. Knowledge of truth is not often reached by the processes of reason. It is due to a spiritual insight.

This present unGodly world makes you an economic slave. Economic freedom is the first step back to being God living in God Country. This means, the less you need and want, your economic burdens decrease; thus the more complete you become. The more you need and want, your economic burdens increase, and the less complete you become.

If you take the time to reflect, you may observe that this unGodly world has made you acquire unnatural desires. You may be obsessed and addicted to desires. One desire fulfilled begets another and another and so on.

Notwithstanding the economic slave system created by the unGods, if you are in complete freedom from needs and desires, then you are dependent on nothing. You are in control of your mind and senses.

There are proponents who declare that you rid yourself of all desires; that you live an ascetic and austere life. To this, I will add something that may seem contrary to what is said in all the aforementioned. There is nothing necessarily wrong with desire. The desire for anything is really just the desire for a fuller, richer, and more abundant life. You are as God is, infinite in nature inherently wanting to expand yourself. He cannot expand Himself if you yourself do not. From this perspective, desire is praiseworthy. I would say that the man who does not desire to live more abundantly is abnormal; that it indicates he doesn't know who he is; that it indicates he has not found higher meaning for life; and that he has settled for less – understandable in this unGodly world which beats you down.

As mentioned, desire can be a tempting thing. However, if you turn to your True Self and allow God to express Himself through you, then you do not have any real desires of your own personally. You must know the difference between the desires He instils and the ego's desires. This is a shorter and more direct path.

Daryl Chang

If you recall, in the early part of life, I had asked myself, "Why do I desire the things I do? Where do my desires come from?" I know not why but I have had this everlasting desire to end the madness here; and to restore the kingdom of God/Love/Heaven physically back to Earth. It may seem silly, magnanimous, and preposterous but I have actually always pondered how I could accomplish this. Now I realize that God is within and so is His kingdom. With this new self-discovery and revelation, I have a deep earnest desire to help all souls, my brothers and sisters, recognize God within themselves too. This desire gave birth to a subsequent desire to write this book; a desire to effectively express this truth in a way that is easily understood by all.

I no longer question where my desires come from. I now know that God put these desires in me, as I'm sure he's put some in you too. I tell you this to affirm I understand the nature of desire so that you can more readily relate and affirm for yourself the same. It is me allowing God to express Himself through me. Recall, a desire is nothing more than the thought of fulfillment seen through an object, entity, or experience. It is finished.

CHAPTER 25
Judgment

♦

At times, God seems like a paradox.

On the one hand, God does not judge. If God judged me, He would be judging Himself. Imagine if He did and He judged things bad, evil, or wrong – life would cease. Besides, He can't; He doesn't have an ego or personality that divides Himself into facets of good and evil, right and wrong, perfect and imperfect. He is whole – *One*.

On the other paradoxical hand, God does judge. Remember, giving and receiving are the same. What I give to others, I give to myself; and what I give to myself, I give to others. So if I give "bad" to others, I get "bad" in return. So technically, for a result to occur, an intrinsic judgment is being made of an action. From this, it is evident that Judgment Day is occurring every moment in my life. This is why I have to be vigilant with what I am thinking, saying, and feeling. This is why it is better when I am in a state of no-thought, non-judgment, non-attachment, and non-resistance.

If an unGod is trying to exercise harm over me, then I may use more diplomatic terms such as distinguishing, discerning, or discriminating his actions, but essentially, I am making a judgment of his intention. But this is neither a good nor proper comparison or explanation of the significance of the word judgment.

Judgment is an effect of having a desire you're attached to. You desire something. Consequently you have expectations. You make a judgment of "good" when a situation is aligned with your expectations or "bad" when it is not aligned.

Judgment is a sign that you do not understand Oneness; you are lesser of love.

People confuse judgment with wisdom. As the world uses the term, you are capable of "good" and "bad" judgment. You have naïvely learnt your personal growth is strengthened by the former and minimized by the latter. There is considerable confusion as to what constitutes good or bad judgment. One person can judge something "good" while another can judge that same something as "bad". Further, the same person will claim showing "good" judgment at one time and at a later time, admit that it was "bad" judgment. There is no consistent criterion for determining what these categories mean. "Good" judgment does not mean anything as does "bad".

Remember how many times you made a judgment with the facts you had and how wrong you were. Would you admit to such an experience? Would you know how many times you thought you were right without ever realizing you were wrong? Why would you make decisions on such an arbitrary basis? Wisdom is not judgment. Wisdom is the relinquishment of judgment.

You are meeting your friend for lunch at 12:00pm. It is now 12:30pm. You get angry because you judge her to be inconsiderate and disrespectful of your time. Perhaps instead you become worried because you judge that possibly she got into an accident as she is always punctual. You cannot judge because you do not know everything.

You have worked hard for the realization of an opportunity you truly desire. Your desire is not fulfilled. You are extremely disappointed because you judge that another such opportunity is not possible. One week later, you encounter an opportunity far better than the one you sought and had thought possible. You cannot judge because you do not know everything.

There is a well known fable you might have heard of already. The story goes as such. An old man and his son worked on a small farm with only one horse to pull the plough. One day, the horse ran away. "How terrible, what bad luck," sympathized the neighbours. The farmer replied, "Bad luck, good luck. Who knows?" A week later, the horse returned from the mountains leading five mares into the barn. "What wonderful luck!" said the neighbours. The old man answered, "Good luck, bad luck. Who knows?" The next day, the son, trying to tame one of the horses, fell and broke his leg. "How terrible. What bad luck!" exclaimed the neighbours. The farmer shrugged and replied, "Bad luck, good luck. Who's to say?" Then the army came to all the farms to take young men to war but the farmer's son was of no use to them, so he was spared. "What good luck!" the neighbours cried out. The old man replied, "Good luck, bad luck? We'll see."

Everything is always working in elegant precision and unfaltering intelligence for your good. God is all-knowing and you the human of limited mind are not. He is always working for your good as He should be because He is you and you are Him. Why would He be directing Himself to "bad" experiences? With this awareness, you realize not only should you not judge, but that you cannot.

Judgment as you've come to perceive it is impossible. You must recognize this. This is not an opinion but a fact. In order for you to judge anything accurately, you would have to be fully aware of everything. You would have to foresee all the effects of your judgments on everyone and everything thereon. Are you able to say that you can do this?

Only God knows all the facts, past, present, and future. Only He knows all the effects of His judgment on everyone and everything involved in any way. And He is wholly fair to everyone for there is no distortion in His perception.

In giving up judgment, you are merely giving up what you did not have. You believe you are giving up something important but you have actually become more honest. When you recognize that judgment is always impossible for you, you no longer attempt it. Where there is no judgment, there is no guilt and shame. Therefore, judge no more.

It is actually easy to relinquish judgment. You think it's difficult because it's just your habit. When you reflect on how much judgment costs you, you will abandon it instantly. Judgment results in pain, sorrow, anger, ugliness, hopelessness, despair, fear, and all sorts of negative feelings. When you give up judgment, it is quite a relief. Your sense of care and attachment disappears. When you do this, you free yourself of a great burden. That is, you acquire peace. You have chosen to trust in God's judgment instead of your own. You are divinely guided and protected.

"What is the easiest way to remove judgments from my thinking?" I can hear you ask. Remind yourself that God is within you; that God is you; and that God does not judge. If you haven't assimilated these aspects wholly yet, then become aware of your feelings and thoughts that produced the judgments. Through this awareness, you will teach yourself to be more refined in your thinking.

When you understand Oneness and are in full awareness of it, you are able to fully recognize yourself in others. When you are able to fully recognize your Oneness, then you will recognize that the bad, the wrong of others is also in you. When you can accept yourself and forgive yourself, you will no longer feel the need to judge and will automatically accept and forgive others.

Once you know who you are, God, you will no longer be quick to judge. You will see that your limited human self who you thought you were before, is not able to judge because it does not know all. When you begin to assimilate the truth of who you are, you will gradually become less and less judgmental until you are no more. You will see God in all.

CHAPTER 26
Sin and Forgiveness
♦

If you wholly understand who you are and judgment as described in the last chapter, then hopefully understanding and surrendering sin and forgiveness should not be difficult since both are based upon judgment.

Sin and forgiveness are constructs of the limited human mind. Both are indications that you have not given up judgment. You think sin and forgiveness are real because you are making judgments of good and evil. You still are not conscious of who you are.

The churches emphasize the Ten Commandments, giving the impression that they are the laws of God when there is only one. When you are as God is, you will not produce such disharmonies. Refraining from these commandments does not mean you "do God", live Godly, or are God. If you are the God that you are, you will automatically refrain from doing these unnatural things.

Ignorance is the cause of all sin. You can say ignorance is the greatest sin. Ignorance is disregard and lack of consciousness both of God, the Creative Principle and your relation to God, the Creative Principle.

A sin has come to mean an action that is judged to be reprehensible, particularly against religious or moral law. A religion makes you believe a sin is a human violation against God's law. A sin is a human judgment of "bad" and is improperly used as a justification for punishment.

A sin is not an act of God but a perceived human one against God. A sin is not recognized by God and has no religious context. A sin occurs when there is an absence of love. To recognize sin means you have forgotten God, the natural power of love, and of who you are.

A sin is an error in how you see, know, and perceive the world around you, your reality. A sin is any thought or feeling that is not of God.

A belief in sin is a sign that you do not understand who you are – *God.*

God is but love, and therefore so are you. You are as God created you. When you are fully conscious of this, you will recognize that love should be and is your natural being. When you are not fully conscious of this, meaning you have forgotten who you are, you will perceive what you term "sin" as justifiable.

When you make it the habit to remember who you are and the love that you are, the world of sinning that is filled with fear, hatred, darkness, violence, poverty, and all negativity will no longer make sense to you. That world will dissolve. A world filled of love instead will become more familiar and home to you because you become more aligned with God, that of love.

Forgiveness is a human creation based on judgment and hence a need to justify the judgment. Forgiveness is a sign that you have not given up judgment. You who would not forgive must judge, for you must justify your failure to forgive. When you judge others, you are judging yourself.

If you believe that someone has wronged you, you withhold forgiveness like it was a gift that you believe the other doesn't deserve. If it is a precious gift that you hold, then why do you feel inner conflict, pain, and suffering? Is it fair that you should feel such if the sin is not yours? You think he is separate from you and has no influence on your thoughts, nor yours on his. Yet, he holds power over you, your thoughts and your feelings.

If you recall the discussion on flow, that of giving and receiving, you will remind yourself that what you give to others you give to yourself. If you forgive another begrudgingly, with the air that you are a better person to someone lower than you, then you have gifted him but not to yourself. You still have not been released from the perceived sin; you are not at peace. If you truly forgive the sin, you will be at peace for giving is receiving.

When you recognize oneness and see your fellow human being as part of that oneness, you see yourself in them. When you recognize yourself as God created you, you forgive because of the love you are. At the same time, you recognize that forgiveness was never required because giving up judgment rendered it meaningless.

When you wholly accept and know who you are, you no longer see a person, a human personality who is doing something bad, evil, or wrong; or who is committing a sin. You forgive him. Instead, you see a soul, a divine child, who is trying to learn to walk; who is crawling, standing, and stumbling; and who is developing. You see no sin; and recognize that forgiveness is not required or is non-existent.

Daryl Chang

CHAPTER 27
Life

♦

I have always felt funerals to be an odd thing. It is the same feeling I had when I first visited an emergency ward at a hospital. I have yet to observe any other species that congregate to do such things. I felt it unnatural to gather at such settings. I do go to these occasions out of love and respect for friends and family but I don't really care to be there otherwise. Hospitals and funerals, tools of the big unGods, prey on the unconscious and their deception of themselves. All involved are pawns of the UnGod's schemes.

I was once at a funeral for a relative's father. He was over eighty years young and was in poor condition during the months before he passed away. Apparently, the family avoided talking about death and what to do when it happened, so they were scrambling around to make arrangements. I heard common comments of "It was so sudden. He seemed fine not too long ago. We didn't expect it." I overheard numerous conversations amongst those attending of how they had to hurry to purchase a burial plot; how they wished to be buried when their time came; and how to be ready with everything organized so that their funeral was smooth. I marvelled at all these people who were already planning for their death. Instead of living life, they were already living death. The immortal self who has the power of creation through thought was creating his mortal self to prove his death.

There was once a summer when every day at 4:30am, birds would chirp and sing constantly outside my bedroom window. The sun had not risen yet so it was still dark. I wondered, "What are these birds yapping about to each other?" By their tone, I could tell they were discussing the madness of the behaviour they saw of us below when flying. The conversation would last exactly twenty minutes each time when I checked my clock. I found it amusing. Many folks would ask me as they would the birds, "Why do you get up so early in the morning?" I smile and counter silently, "Why do you *not* get up so early in the morning?"

Why does the bird instantly get up from bed at 4:30am with such vitality? Why does the bird not hit the snooze button for ten minutes more of sleep? Why does the bird start its day when the sun hasn't come out yet?

The bird has not been beaten down and defeated by a survival system illegitimately created by the UnGod. He doesn't know about that world and isn't working for a living to get by. Life is not a toil or chore. Life is a wondrous adventure as it should be to only hunger more of. The bird, who is life, is enjoying life as God is.

There is a squirrel I often see in my backyard. Throughout the day, he runs back and forth atop the fence doing who knows what. He's been doing this for years. Except for his physical size that varies, he appears the same as the first day I saw him. You cannot tell its age. They do not appear to "age" as man does. "It's probably not the same squirrel," I can hear you say. You are possibly correct or not. When I observe any part of nature, with variations of their size due to what and how much they eat, they all appear the same throughout its existence. Their vitality is consistent throughout their existence too.

Like the squirrel, if you've ever seen gigantic trees like sequoias, you cannot tell its age. You know it's been growing for a while but you cannot tell for how long they've existed. Except for size, its appearance is the same throughout.

What is the difference between man and all of nature? Again, they do not have an ego, free will, and self-consciousness. They do not think of their own accord. God is their consciousness.

The consciousness in the sun is the same consciousness in the air, in the moon, in the tree, in the bird, in you and in me. The I AM that flows through the sun and the air is the same I AM that flows through you and me. The power and intelligence in the sun and the air is the same as in you and me.

The sun shines with the same vitality every day it rises; the air and wind move with the same vitality every day you greet it; the birds outside my window display the same vitality every day when they sing. Man is the greatest of all creations and yet somehow, we don't exhibit the same vitality each day.

Daryl Chang

What does the sun, the moon, and the tree know that I don't know?

The sun, the moon, and the tree are of God consciousness only. The sun, the moon, and the tree do not know how to die. They only know how to live. The sun, the moon, and the tree never contemplate death.

God is a formless invisible force of energy with supreme vitality. He is eternal and infinite. God is within me. I am one with God. As I've established through consciousness, I, my soul who is also eternal and infinite, never die. All is spiritual; the physical is spiritual manifest. It follows then that the cells, of which I am made of, are immortal. If this is the case, then why do I witness physical death?

Let us begin with the end in mind. That is, that there is no end for we are eternal.

God is all in all. God is perfect good. God is within me. I am one with God. I AM God. I am perfect despite apparently entering an unGodly and imperfect world. Everything down to the cell is perfect. It follows then that if I came into the world that is God Country where perfect conditions exist, I would forever be perfect and live perfectly because that is all I know and that is who I AM.

What then shifts me from my perfect state to an imperfect one?

I am made in the image and likeness of God. I have an ego and free will. I've established that two beings live inside me, God and unGod. I have the superpower to create things and my experiences through my free will and thought. I am able to think with my Lil-i.

If I am conscious, I know Big-I, God, is my True Self and my true Master. Lil-i is the servant to Big-I, God, who is the all-knowing, unlimited, impersonal, and perfect mind. Big-I knows only love, purity, and all things good. He knows that all are one. As such, if Big-I provides the perfect thoughts as He does, and I command Lil-i to follow the direction of these thoughts, then a perfect state is maintained.

If I am unconscious, I do not know Big-I is my True Self and true Master. Instead, Lil-i, my false self, usurps the Master role through an implied consent of my silence. Lil-i is my limited personal imperfect mind. He lets me think that he is me and I am him. Lil-i provides his thoughts as my own. Lil-i who has eaten from the Tree of Knowledge knows not only love, purity, and good things but that of fear, impurity, and not-so-good things. He thinks he is separate from all.

Lil-i can still occasionally think of good things so that I experience good things. This will help keep some semblance of a perfect state. However, when Lil-i thinks of fear, impurity, and not-so-good things, my perfect state begins to shift to a less than perfect one. Maintaining this perfect state is difficult because this unGodly world is still presenting dominant evidence of negative things. Thus, I potentially stray much from my perfect state.

The UnGod and his big unGods have successfully poisoned many minds to think imperfect things; many hearts to feel imperfect things; many eyes to see imperfect things; many ears to hear imperfect things; many lives to live imperfect things.

The big unGods have built systems to remove God from you and thus your perfection. They have built churches to remove your spirituality and consciousness from you. They have built schools posing as education but in reality are prison camps to indoctrinate you with their thoughts and remove the creativity of your own. Without consciousness of your own thought, you are unconscious of your own power. They have built a medical industry, along with hospitals and mental facilities, to deceive you into believing in dis-ease and ill-health. They have built old age residences, long term care facilities, and funeral homes to hoodwink you into believing in aging and death. They have cunningly imprisoned and trapped you in the physical realm to distract you from the spiritual realm. To make sure there are no loose ends, they also trap you in spiritual prisons from your spiritual selves.

The big unGods keep you busy, distracted, overwhelmed, stressed, and in fear so that you have no time to acquire true knowledge; hence wisdom of your spiritual selves.

I ask the question again, "Why do I witness physical death?"

I witness physical death because many do not know who they are; they do not know where they come from and why they are here. When they don't know is when they are the death of this world. They fear death and they know not why. They despise the likes of tyranny, war, poverty, and dis-ease, but that is what they are in their beings. They don't know as the sun, the moon, and the tree knows. You misuse your power to think and create. You believe in death and so you think of death. You manifest this reality.

You are perfect. You do not think or know this true because you don't know who you are. You see, think, and feel with your physical senses. You have been misled to think, see, and feel imperfections from the physical perspective. When you know who you are, you know this is true. This you see with your spiritual eyes; think with your spiritual mind; and feel with your spiritual heart. God is perfect and His kingdom – *Consciousness* – is perfect conditions only.

There is only life for that is what God is. Hence, you are too.

CHAPTER 28
Well-being

♦

There is an old tale from the middle ages where one of the monasteries kept the bones of a saint, renowned for miracles of healing. On certain days, people would line up to touch the relics and all who did so were healed. One night, someone stole the bones from the case they were placed in. The monks did not want to alarm anyone so they kept quiet about it. They hoped they would find the thief and timely recover the bones. They went down to the cellar and dug up the bones of a murderer, which had been buried many years before. They placed them in the case, intending to make a reasonable excuse for why the usual miracles did not happen. They opened the gates next morning to let the crowd in and to their astonishment, the miracles continued to happen.

The healing power was never in the bones. The person was healed by God within because of the intense belief of their healing from it.

I can think of no species where one is dependent on another of its own kind for the survival of its own existence. God has given each creature everything they require to be independent and exist. After growing past a child rearing and nurturing stage, it does not need a teacher type beyond its mother to educate it on further life survival skills. It does not need a doctor type to heal its hurts or ills. It does not need a police type to protect it from societal harm amongst its own kind. It does not need a lawyer type to protect it from a falsely made law amongst its own kind. It does not need a financial advisor to counsel it on attaining things in its life. Only the unconscious man thinks he does. The unconscious man has been conditioned or trained to believe he needs another man outside himself for such things. The UnGod has tricked you. Does it make sense that God would make man, the greatest of all creations, dependent on another of his own kind, especially for his well-being?

As I've established, you are eternal and infinite. Your cells are immortal. Apparently, this has been proven by science but the big unGods ensure that you know not of these reports; and that it does not

Daryl Chang

become prevalent knowledge. Your cells are consciousness so they are also all-knowing. That is, they know of the present and future needs of the whole body and acts accordingly

Life isn't generated by the cells of your body. Life produces your body. God is life. God produces your body. God is eternal, infinite, and perfect. As such, I technically should be ageless and forever youthful. If this is the case, then why do I witness aging and ill-health?

As I described in the last chapter on Life, thought is a significant and primary factor in the shift away from your perfect state toward mortality. I trust it is understood by now that the more you are separated from yourself and who you are, then you become less perfect physically. Let's indulge in other aspects beyond that.

As mentioned, God is a dynamic, moving, ever-flowing force. If this flow of force is restricted or hampered, then its power will become stagnant and reduced ultimately to death.

If air is not allowed to flow, it becomes stagnant. Likewise, if water is not allowed to flow, it too becomes stagnant. This is equivalent to say that if God – *love* – is not allowed to flow through you, then you become stagnant. You will appear aged. You will experience ill-health.

Your unconscious soul is misled and ruled by your ego, the limited human mind, resulting in all your mortal limitations.

Man by his own limited thinking, has constantly dissected everything. So it is with the physical body. They have broken down your mind as consisting of the conscious, subconscious, and Superconscious mind. In reality, there is only one mind. They've broken down your body into multiple systems like the respiratory, digestive, and nervous system. In reality, there is only one system. The divisions were part of a teaching now past. It served its purpose for the time but you must now bring all into accord of the whole.

Signs of aging and ill-health are indications that the body's vitality is being reduced to save it from sudden death and prolong its duration. The intellectual reasoning that you have an immune system is incorrect; and that its strength is pivotal to you combating illness is a fallacy. Your body has merely shifted into a self-preservation mode. Your body is not suicidal. Instead of dropping dead, you die by inches. In the process of slowly dying, you suffer until the body can endure no more to the point of what we term death. The body never ages nor wears. It merely weakens. This is to say that your identification with God, your Father, is gradually being lost.

The UnGod and his big unGods have fooled you into believing the reality of old age and dis-ease for which they are the culprits. They have calculatedly disrupted the flow of God through you, spiritually, mentally, emotionally, and physically. They are the factual cause of age and dis-ease.

Though all things of God are good, this unGodly world has conditioned you to judge things as good or bad. They have also defined for you what is good and bad. They have told you that dis-ease is bad and that you must fight it. A good example is what they have given a label that rhymes with dancer. You accept their toxic treatment and possibly are cured by their criteria. You're happy again but then it comes back. The illness was treated physically but as you now know, the physical is the spiritual manifest. You had not changed spiritually. Your mental and emotional habits were still the same, hence the reoccurrence. You have not made the connection still.

Instead of bad, the illness can be viewed as good. Many will attest to this because God finally got their attention that they were not living rightly. It incited them to change their lifestyle. The dis-ease was an extreme condition that made you turn back to God within yourself. Though this is wonderful, you may remain unconscious of who you are. The spiritual enlightenment is still not complete.

All is spiritual; the physical is spiritual manifest. The two are intermingled, swinging to and fro like a pendulum. Poor spiritual nourishment will result in poor physical manifestation. Poor physical nourishment will cause further detriment spiritually and physically. When you tackle a physical illness through physical means such as natural supplements and nutritious food, it will surely help. However, it is not addressing the spiritual cause and so the benefits will not be long lasting.

The modern day medicine takes this approach. If you have a dis-ease, then you will be advised to undergo treatment with their drugs and tactics. You will be told you are cured by their fictitious measurements. Some time later, the dis-ease reoccurs. You have not changed who you are so the physical manifestation of the dis-ease reappears. Your limited human mind has not thought to go beyond the physical realm. The big unGods have conditioned you to stay there.

The big unGods have preyed on your wholly unconscious soul to believe in the power of their man-made medicine, concoctions, and chemical solutions to save you. You are mistaken. These are all fabrications to sicken, dehumanize, and enslave you further. God requires no such unnatural thing to be put inside you or Him in order to heal yourself or Himself or to prevent some illness. He is God. You are God. All creatures are God. All of nature is God. God has given you (and all His creations) everything you need within to keep you eternal and infinite. You have the power to heal yourself and others.

The big unGods of this world attack you from all dimensions: spiritually, mentally, emotionally, and physically. They have you focused on the physical realm so they poison you physically as an effective means. They pollute the air, food, and water so your well-being is no more. This constant assault destroys the perfect cells of your physical body to malfunction. When you are in pain, you cannot think or feel straight. They are very clever. They persistently weaken your mind to reduce greatly the possibility that you venture within yourself. They know that their power and false kingdom will collapse should you ever discover the truth of who you are; discover the power you have; discover God, the true God, and His kingdom.

CHAPTER 29
The Path

♦

When a seed is planted in fertile ground, it soon emerges to indicate to the world its existence. It is in full God consciousness throughout its entire physical existence. It progresses through development stages eventually to blossom into its grandest of expression.

When a baby is born from a fertilized egg, it is in full God consciousness. A mother does not have to instruct herself to develop the baby before she gives birth. God makes this happen without anyone technically hampering the process. Only when the baby finally exits the mother's womb does the capability for self-consciousness begin.

In the early stages, the baby is nearer to full God consciousness despite its external environment. If the external environment was God Country, the baby would manifest who he is perfectly. Alas, its present environment is unGodly thereby tainting his self-consciousness of his God self. His ego develops influenced greatly by his surrounding environment. Unless his parents are conscious beings, he will start to increasingly lose his God self. The longer it takes for him to recognize God, the more he will have to regain his self-consciousness and his God self. The entire process is essentially a game or a school test, if you will. It is only by mastering the game or excelling the test that he will blossom into the grandest of his unique expression, as the flower did when it started its life journey.

When I am in the right frame of mind, I am truly conscious of being God Himself. I see the spiritual souls of children for who they are. I see each human being as a child, not clouded by the physical masks they wear but the spiritual beings that are unseen. They are like the physical babies that must go through the process of learning and growing.

When you see a child, your nature softens. You are filled with joy by its existence. You are patient with their struggles to learn and grow. You are caring and nurturing to help them become great human beings.

Daryl Chang

You are supportive of what they want to do and become. You are affectionate because they are a part of you. You love them because that is who you are. You love them just because.

I see with my spiritual eyes divine beings floating around, not physical human beings walking around. I see souls of children going through the growing pains of learning to become a Higher Self of God standards not the physical adults conforming to society standards – they simply need proper guidance, love, and nurturing. I hear with my spiritual ears, souls of baby talk that are incomprehensible in God Country, the abusive, senseless, and negative words of society. I taste with my spiritual tongue, the soul sweetness of the divine beings they are, not the physical bitterness of their spiritual ignorance. I feel with my spiritual heart love, not anger or annoyance.

God is all in all. That is the Law of One. God is One. You and I and all of our brothers and sisters and all the creatures and creations of this world are one. When you recognize all is one, you will begin to recognize God in another. You will begin to look beyond the physical mask worn and see the soul of a child of God that is unseen. Then, you who had not known who you are will begin to become or rather, be who you are: *God.*

When you start for the light of God Country, you must forsake and forget the land of the UnGod – *hell.* You cannot go and stay at the same time. You must forsake the old and adhere to the new. You must forget the things you do not wish to remember and remember only the things you wish to retain. One is as essential as the other. If you wish your vision to be fulfilled, then the vision only must be remembered. You must remember by holding in mind the vision you wish to reproduce. You must disremember or refuse to remember the thing you do not wish to reproduce. In order to bring forth the vision, every idea, thought, word, or act must be true to it. This is true concentration, the concentration of devotion, the centering of the forces upon the essential. This is loving the ideal. It is only through love that an ideal can be given expression. Love makes the ideal become the real.

The UnGod was clever when he came up with the catchy idiom, "Ignorance is bliss," because for him, it's true. He conveniently omitted the word 'your' and 'my' – *Your ignorance is my bliss* – from the idiom so that the unconscious souls wouldn't catch on. Insulting them personally this way might have shortened his game.

Your ego is a bastard tenant who deliberately violates you and lives rent free in your cozy abode. If you had a bad tenant, you would for certain evict him immediately. The ego has made you put on a lot of dead weight of beliefs, dogma, and superstitions. Something or someone like Jesus is not going to come along, place you in a pram, push and walk you around till you miraculously lose the weight raising you to a higher plane. I'm sorry if this crushes your fantasy but only you can and must do the work.

So if you say "I'm tired of being angry; tired of all this war; tired of not having true freedom," then mean it. There is a higher life beyond this tedious struggle for existence that the UnGod has made you believe life is. The path seems long and hard but may actually be short and easy. However, you will never know this if you prefer to continue engaging with the UnGod you are familiar with rather than the God you *really* don't know yet. Your desire to change must be greater than your desire to stay the same. You must have a deep willingness. You must not hesitate. You must decide to do the work, then do it. Become immaculate and honourable with your word. You must not only know the path but walk the path. Then you will be free.

Always focus on the cure, never the problem.

Things are not brought into being by thinking about their deemed opposites. Health is never to be attained by studying dis-ease and thinking about dis-ease; righteousness is not to be promoted by studying sin and thinking about sin; and no one ever got rich by studying poverty and thinking about poverty.

Medicine as a science of dis-ease has increased dis-ease. Religion as a science of sin has promoted sin, and economics as a study of poverty has filled the world with wretchedness and want.

If you want to become abundant, you must not make a study of poverty. Do not talk about poverty. Do not investigate it or concern yourself with it. Never mind what its causes are. You have nothing to do with them; nor dis-ease and all of the UnGod's conceptions.

When you enter into full and constant mental relations with health, wealth, and all things love, you must of necessity cease all relationship with its counterpart. Enter into complete thought connection with perfection. Things outside God Country are totally unnatural. See and

Daryl Chang

feel only those things in God Country. This is your way back home. This is right thinking. This is who you are.

I find that the path to God Country is uncrowded and untrodden. I meet people along the way as I travel in the other direction they're going. I'm quite willing to have a deep intimate conversation; to share what I've discovered; and to possibly make new friends who will accompany me. I realize most like to discuss nothing other than the distractions of the UnGod's world. If by chance I'm able to express some of what I've shared with you in these few pages, I'm often met with perplexed and confused faces as it doesn't seem to make sense to them; granted, I don't always explain things clearly in such a short time. I too, am a bit perplexed myself by my experiences. They will admit that the world is not right and that they do not like it. Yet they will not pause to consider what they themselves can do to help correct it. They shrug their shoulders and accept their reality. The oppressors and the slaves are co-operators in unconsciousness, and while they seem to afflict each other, are in reality afflicting themselves. I respect the path their souls take as I do mine; so I leave them alone and allow them to evolve according to their own needs and designs. I continue walking in solitude, willing to give when one is willing to receive.

I've come to a realization. There's a familiar quote that says, "There is not one path. There is not even the right path. There is only your path." You can only be who you are, not someone else. No one can teach you of your God self – not even Jesus or Buddha or any other teacher. They can teach you only of theirs. To fulfil your "destiny", you must become who you are and what you uniquely are. You'll never become that if you try to live according to another's life plan or direction. The only way you will come to understand who you are and this fire that lives within you is through the truth of your own understanding and guidance of your own God self. Only you can know what experience is needed in your soul for your own fulfillment. I am merely pointing you the way as others have done for me.

When you do your inner work, it is void of external gratification society has made you accustomed to wanting. You must do everything yourself. You must encourage yourself. You must stroke your own ego. You must compliment yourself. You must praise yourself for how far you've come and for a job well done. You must approve of your own self. You may possibly perceive this challenging because there is no one around but yourself to know and cheer you on and say, "Look at what you've done. I'm so proud of you." But you are mistaken. God is with you all the time. He sees you. He knows what you are doing and how you are carrying yourself. It is evident or will be evident that He is joyous and proud of you because He rewards you with all good things and everything.

CHAPTER 30
Back Home

♦

Have you ever had the fortune to be completely immersed in nature where you are surrounded only by mountains, trees, water, stars, and an open sky of darkness and/or light? You see and hear only God because that is all there is when untouched by an unGodly man. UnGod does not exist here. Words cannot and will not describe the feelings and experience. I am forever in deep admiration, appreciation, and amazement by the sense of awe, beauty, and silence that envelops me.

I sometimes have trouble organizing the things I have to do in my daily life. But every day, here is God creating, coordinating, and managing all of life. He makes the sun come up, the water flow, the wind blow, the birds fly, and the fish swim. Nothing is too big and too small. Everything is important. He even makes time for me. He makes my hair grow, my lungs breathe, and my blood circulate. How great is He?

I can do the same because He is me, and I am Him. But not quite yet. I first have to get through kindergarten. So much more to learn than what I've written in this book but I have time. I'm eternal and infinite.

You will not appreciate the aforementioned if you live in a concrete jungle city where instead you are surrounded by skyscrapers, tall buildings, cell towers, antennae, shopping malls, cars, roads, and all things man-made. If you are born there and never ventured outside, you will not have a glimpse of God Country. You see and hear only UnGod because God is drowned out. There are sirens, horns, traffic, television, music, chatter, and relentless noise. To see and hear God temporarily, you will have to create a semblance of your own little God Country within this unGodly world.

I remember in my first year at university residence, I had a roommate I did not choose. The residence assigned him to the room we shared. He was apparently a smart guy for while I studied often in the room, I never saw him study much. He would frequently come back in the night 1:00-2:00am and disrupt my sleep. He burned incense which filled the room with an aroma that made me nauseous. He had a peculiar body odour that made me queasy. He was a person that was in my life by no choice of mine.

The semester finally ended and so did the roommate accommodation. Later, I moved to a new place never to see him again. He was no longer in my consciousness. He no longer existed to me. This is because I made a choice of where I wanted to be.

And so it is with the UnGod of this world. When I took up residence here, it was not by choice. The choice was made for me. Now, I have a choice as you do. I choose a new home to live. I emigrated and now reside in God Country. I am admittedly still tied to the UnGod's world because of the long-standing intricacies of his sophisticated schemes. I work less for the UnGod and his fake currencies of money and its cousins. The longer I stay in God Country, the old fades. Like my initial roommate, I no longer have to tolerate, accommodate, or interact with him. He is gradually disappearing from my consciousness.

I do not deny the existence of the UnGod because to deny it means that I have to acknowledge its existence. Instead, I raise my thoughts above the false UnGod. He is nothing but a false idea. He does not exist. I simply let him go.

I work for God only and His true currencies of love, wisdom, and power. I fix my thoughts and attention steadfastly on God and God Country. There exists nothing outside it.

When you live in God Country where only God lives, you don't know that UnGod exists; where there is only love, joy, peace and good things only, you don't know that fear, sorrow, turmoil, and not-so-good things exist; where everything is provided for you in abundance, you don't know that scarcity and poverty exist; where there is vitality in everyone, you don't know that dis-ease, aging, and death exist; where there is respect, care, and cooperation, you don't know what war, conflict, and disputes are.

If you do not find yourself in God Country, remind yourself that it is because you are still thinking with your limited human mind, the Lil-i. If you wish to gain admittance and enter God Country, you will need love as your passport; and you must leave your ego and personality

Daryl Chang

outside the front door like the drenched umbrella and muddied galoshes after a hard rainfall.

This is how it is naturally. You are naturally a good person – *you are God*. If you live in a ghetto – an unGodly environment – where there are prevalent gangs living a criminal lifestyle, you are more susceptible to becoming a gangster yourself, doing not-so-good things. If you are unconscious and not true to yourself, you do become a gangster – the UnGod. However, if you are conscious and are true to yourself, you become a saint – *God*. It is better when you don't live in a ghetto – the UnGod's false world (hell). You are no longer susceptible or tempted by a thug lifestyle.

In God Country, there is lots of sunshine throughout the day. In fact, it is always full of light here, seldom if any a cloudy day. There is not much darkness of sufferings and disharmonies. Do you ever pause to notice the effect sunshine has on you? I do. I am in a more uplifting mood; I have more get-up-and-go; and I want to go about and do things. Contrast that with a dark cloudy day where the sun is blocked. It makes for a dreary day. God is generally always in a joyous mood. Nonetheless, I, my reverted human self, am not in a typical uplifting mood; I have less get-up-and-go; and I want to stay inside and laze.

This is the same with sunshiny people – people of light. When I am around sunshiny people, I feel happier; I have more energy; and I want to do things with them. When I'm around not-so-sunshiny people, I feel dreary; I have less energy; and I prefer not to do things with them. Here in God Country, everyone is young, beautiful, wise, powerful, and all-loving.

It is no wonder then that the big unGods mislead you to think the sun is bad for you. It is no surprise that the big unGods manipulate and darken the weather. It is no shock that the big unGods endlessly try to remove the light within you.

Light is information and energy. You are light; you are positive; you are God. When you are lesser light, you are negative; you are UnGod. Be the light not the darkness. When you are here in God Country, you can't help but be bright and radiant like the sun. God within you is the highest teacher and the sole authority of you for He is the light which lights every man that enters the world. You are His light that lights the heart candle of every soul behind the mask of a human personality; that disperses any darkness of egos; and that shines and radiates warmth to those around.

When I fully establish myself in God Country, I intend to fill my days of its physical realization with playing many sports, particularly hockey, billiards, scrabble, chess, reading, writing, painting, listening to music and silence, dancing, hiking, carpentry, arts and crafts, building stuff, learning to play a musical instrument, cooking and baking, gardening, landscaping, having good conversations, smiling, laughing, hugging, napping, sun gazing, indulging in my creative desires, contemplating, and endless communing with God.

Occasionally, when I'm out and about exploring, I will venture down the path and make a wrong turn somewhere where things are obviously not right, a place once familiar. When this happens, I just turn around and make my way back home. I know I'm home when it feels like home. When I'm home, there's a warm and loving feeling. There's calmness, serenity, and peace. There is no angst, fear, worry, or stress of any kind. It's a wonderful place. It's not far a walk to go back home. In fact, it takes no time at all really.

You're welcome to come visit me anytime. Whenever you'd like to, just let me know. I'll make us some hot cacao. We can sit by my cozy fireplace and have us a nice deep intimate conversation. I'll be here waiting to welcome you with open arms; to tell you how I've missed you; to help you set up permanent residency here with me if you'd like.

I look for forward to an encounter with you but if not, I wish you a good life. All the love, all the wisdom, and all the power to you.

CHAPTER 31
Advancement

♦

It helps to know you are making progress when walking down the path to God Country. You need signs that suggest you are making advancement toward what you aim to be. I've composed a list for you that I trust will help you notice your journey.

- You smile as soon as you wake up in the morning because you recognize you're alive.
- You smile a lot.
- You think less.
- You trust the universe more.
- Your perception, intelligence, and wisdom are enhanced somehow.
- You spontaneously smile, chuckle, giggle, or laugh for no apparent reason.
- You see people in a different light.
- You observe people's egos with a new perspective.
- You no longer feed your ego or the ego of others.
- You no longer react to negativity (ie. people, events, situations, environment, results, et cetera).
- You no longer overreact.
- You accept things more readily.
- You tend to judge less and appreciate circumstances, situations, and experiences as is.
- You are grateful for anything and everything. You are in gratitude always.
- You feel more at peace.
- You become kinder and more loving without apparent effort.
- You harmonize your heart and brain towards what feels like your truth, your purpose.
- You find courage to act.

- You identify less and less with any thing: an object, an idea, a person, a role, a job, a title, a label, a class, a category, a type, an age, a group, a religion, a country, et cetera.
- You notice that you seem to be at the right place at the right time more often.
- You luck out more often.
- You just do your thing.
- You're possibly told you have a certain inexplicable glow about you.

CHAPTER 32
Reflection

◆

It is in the simplicity of a profound expression as it is in the profundity of a simple expression, whether it be an idea, a thought, a word, a moment, or an object, that therein lies the beauty of it.

I'd like to share a poem with you. I trust you enjoy it.

Reflection

Sitting on the grass,
I look out into the meadow.
Butterflies flutter all around
To where the flowers grow.

Even from where I am,
I can smell their sweet fragrance.
I spot a chrysanthemum, I think
And a blue monarch by chance.

The flower beckons
With its alluring red.
The butterfly notices
And forges ahead.

She lands on the petals
And is greeted with a smile.
But she quickly departs
After only a short while.

As I now gaze at the flower
Focused on its entirety,
It's only then I notice
Its formal true beauty.

Not because of its colour,
Not because of its smell.
There's something beyond that
As far as I can tell.

There's a quiet humility
It knows about its being.
Not forcing anything,
Not even intentionally doing.

It knows its purpose,
It knows its rootedness.
It doesn't question
Its connectedness.

It wants nothing of itself,
It doesn't see itself from life.
It is one with what life wants,
And so there is no strife.

Once you remain still
With a certain degree of presence
And enhanced perception,
You can sense the inner essence.

Until this happens
Most will just see the outer form.
And without any awareness,
You will believe that is the norm.

As I reflect upon it further,
I realize in this life game
We are as the flower,
Together we are the same.

If we really look at existence,
It has enough to offer.
Live in the present now,
That much we must honour.

I no longer question,
I have become knowing.
As knowing as a human spirit,
Is capable of becoming.

I am the joy and happiness,
I am without a wish.
I experience everything,
It is quite delish.

CHAPTER 33
The Way

♦

I have come to a close of the book.

Your false self, Lil-i, has dominated your thinking and your feelings for quite some time now. Your human personality and intellect will doubt the words in this book because its life is threatened. It is afraid of no longer being the master of you. When you find the faith and courage to go beyond its cynicism, you will progress to a point of joy one day.

I'd like to encapsulate the essence of the knowledge shared with you. I trust it will help preserve clarity for you.

Cast off all personal beliefs and opinions that you have gathered because of your false self. Have consciousness of God's Presence within you. Acknowledge you are one with Him. Accept every fellow human being is one with you and Him as well.

Know God is the final authority to whom you can turn to directly and immediately always. He is the one and only true Master. He is all-knowing. Anyone who claims to be a master is self-ordained and nothing more nor less than a human personality.

Cease looking to any authority, teachings and religions, coming from an outer source – no matter how wonderful the truths and wisdom they speak. Indulge no more in occult societies and more spiritual attainment for this is of the ego and human personality.

Understand that God is the Intelligence in everything, from the tiniest cell to the largest sun. Recognize that you need no mediator between you and God – not even Jesus for He was merely demonstrating and teaching this truth.

Make time to be still and go into the silence often. Learn to commune with God and hear His still small voice. Be willing to receive His wisdom as He is willing to give it.

Be conscious of your breathing always. Feel, embrace, and bathe in His Presence flowing through you.

See with your spiritual eyes always that God is ONE and is ALL, and that all is good only. Realize that unless you see God in everything, you cannot see good in anything. See through the eyes of Love to dispel imperfections you see with your limited human self.

Think only of love and perfection; do not think of fear and imperfections. See both yourself and a person as successful and perfect; do not see yourself and a person with failures and imperfections. See only well-being, abundance, and peace; do not see ill-health, poverty, and conflict. Live an impersonal life void of personal values and free of your human personality; do not live a personal life full of personal values and enslaved to your human personality.

Rise above the world; do not sink below the world. Rise above your ego and personality and that of others; do not sink to your ego and personality and that of others. See beneath a human mask, an invisible divine soul of unlimitedness; do not see the surface of a human mask, a visible human personality of personal limitations. See with the eyes of God; do not see with the eyes of man.

God has reserved for you thoughts and teachings which are yours and yours only, and which He will give you in secret – when you are ready to receive them. Allow Him to work through you so that you blossom an aspect of natural intelligence that has never been expressed before.

You alone are your greatest friend, lover, and teacher for only you know what the best of all things is for you. Turn to Your True Self, God within, for all answers to all questions. He is the Supreme Teacher to gain oneness with God. Here you enter God Consciousness.

You will only know God when you experience the realization of God within yourself. Simply *know*.

Epilogue

◆

This unGodly world is upside-down so it is no wonder that many in it work backwards. They try to have more things, or make more money, in order to do more of what they want, so they will be happier. The way it actually works is the reverse. They must first be who they are, then do what they need to do, in order to have what they want.

We selfishly live our lives thinking what is good for us is good for the world. We are mistaken. We must change how we live, what we do, and make sure it is good for the world and then it follows it will be good for us.

I have envisioned a more beautiful world for quite some time because I believe the world I came into is not as it could be or should be. I used to think and feel like I was alone in this vision but as time progressed, I recognize that there are quite a few others who share similar views. And so, it does not feel as overwhelming or hopeless as it once did when I felt I was tackling it on by myself. I will do as I can.

Can you envision a world full of love, joy, peace, happiness, and compassion because the collective human consciousness has risen to such heights that we no longer unconsciously create wars, poverty, pollution, and consciously take true stewardship of the planet as God gave us? I can. I do. The very thought makes me smile.

Sharing of anything, of everything, particularly knowledge, not sole accumulation, contributes to wisdom, wealth, health, and happiness. I have written this book for this purpose. I thank you for taking the time to read it. I trust you find it invaluable in your spiritual development.

No matter what we possess, we are poor when we do not have well-being. When you have experienced the efficacy of something, it is appropriate to tell others about it. All things in our world, God's world, are a birthright not to be commoditized or monetized.

Daryl Chang

Nothing better is possible until we cease to be unconscious. This can only come about by the rise of each individual of the collective human race to a higher viewpoint. And this can only come about by the rise of such individuals here and there as are ready for the higher viewpoint. *You are one such individual.* When you begin to better understand God and to live consciously, you will recognize that chance encounters do not exist in the universe. God is always working with elegant precision and unfaltering intelligence. This is here for your learning experience if you choose to use it. The fact that you have picked up this book means that you are open to what God has to offer you.

Would you be willing to accept that our purpose and destiny is to bring a new dimension into this world by living in conscious oneness with the totality and conscious alignment with universal intelligence?

Are you willing to act with importance and urgency and to strive for that level of consciousness where we cooperate for the highest good and serve humanity, animals, and nature?

Are you willing to lift your awareness, recognize the underlying truth, and start making conscious changes to play an uphill joyous game instead?

We are all part of the Divine, and when we recognize this, we will learn to lovingly share, care, and help one another. I would like you to pioneer with me the path to God Country for all. Let's be willing to try so that the world is better. Or not. I am willing to try. I trust you are too. Shall we get on with it then? I'm in joy for I can hear you say, "Yes."

Visuals

ONENESS

GALAXY
made up of # solar systems

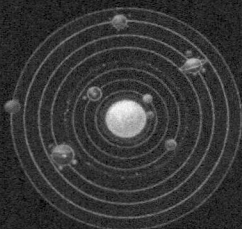

SOLAR SYSTEM
made up of # planets

PLANET
made up of # human beings and
other creatures of nature

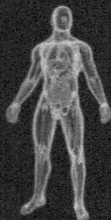

HUMAN BEING
made up of # cells

CELL
made up of # atoms

"*The kingdom of God is within you.*"

LUKE 17:21

THE KINGDOM OF GOD

THERE EXISTS ONLY • YOU SEE/FEEL ONLY

oneness life (eternity) perfection

calmness joy peace health

happiness beauty youth harmony

bund nce love compassion lightness

ratitude expansion inclusion

kindness

ourity connectedness stillness

wholeness unlimitedness power

freedom non-attachment

non-judgment goodness

non-resistance

"Whatever you have in mind, do it, for God is with you."
Chronicles 17:2
✦

"Be still and know that I am God."
Psalms 46:10
✦

"For I know the plans I have for you; Plans to prosper you and not to
harm you, plans to give you hope and a future."
Jeremiah 29:11
✦

"Seek first the kingdom of God and His righteousness,
and all these things shall be added to you."
Matthew 6:33
✦

"I can of mine own self do nothing."
John 5:30
✦

"I am the door. If anyone enters by me, he will be saved."
John 10:9
✦

"I and My Father are one."
John 10:30
✦

"You are gods; you are all sons of the Most High."
John 10:34
✦

"I am the resurrection and the life.
Whoever believes in me will live, even though he dies."
John 11:25
✦

"I am the way, the truth, and the life;
no one comes to the Father except through me."
John 14:6
✦

O nce upon a time, there was a Zen master looking for good disciples. He became frustrated because the ones he had usually gave themselves over to avarice, envy, gluttony, or sloth. He asked himself, "Who is my true disciple?" As he meditated one day, he realized, "Ah, a baby must be pure." He took care of an abandoned baby and provided everything the child needed. Fourteen years later, the master thought, "I need to take a shopping trip. I'll take the boy." Before they set out on their trip, the master said to the boy, "Don't be attracted to lions." The boy asked, "What's a lion?" to which the master replied, "long mane, fair skin, red lips, flowing gait." The boy not fully understanding remarked, "Oh." As the two strolled through the village, the boy exclaimed, "This market is fun!" The master decided to let the boy explore on his own and said before parting, "Come back here at dusk. Don't be attracted to lions." "I won't," the boy replied. When the two met up at dusk, the master asked, "What did you buy?" The boy replied, "Nothing." "What did you want to buy?" the master asked. "I don't dare tell you," the boy hesitantly replied. "Tell me, don't be afraid," the master said reassuringly. The boy feeling encouraged said, "Master, I want a lion. I'd like to be eaten by a lion." The master put his palm to his forehead and uttered, "Oh my disciple."

God is within me as He is in you. Oftentimes, something simple yet unfathomable is not so easy to accept as true especially amidst the noise and distractions of the current world. But this is just a habit from your limited thinking because you are not conscious of who you are yet. This is the irony of your current predicament. Deep down, you will admit you have always felt or known that something is not quite right. You have been conditioned to dismiss what you know in the depths of your soul. God within you is always urging you to free yourself from those who keep you in their ball and chain, including your false self. Your intuition is like any muscle; it needs to be exercised to gain personal strength.

You will soon perceive that there is a higher life for the God-born so-called human being. To be born and mired into a human existence of man-made laws, dogma, superstitions, and conventions through which you struggle is unnatural. You have been cleverly misled and deceived long enough now. Once you truly understand your true being, the struggles you have falsely created will dissolve. The UnGod, the big unGods, and all unGods will no longer be able to intimidate, manipulate, and enslave you. You will learn to live in harmony with God and nature and a sense of well-being will return.

In the light of the true understanding of who you are, you do not need a king, a queen, a pope, a priest, a prime minister, a healer, a teacher, a saviour or an authority. You, in true perception, are the king, the queen, the pope, the priest, the prime minister, the healer, the teacher, the saviour, the authority; none but yourself and God stand alone.

This book is here now to help you remember what you have always known. Read this book slowly and intently. Read with your heart and feel what the words mean to you rather than trying to understand them intellectually. Little by little, or maybe immediately, you'll discover something of life-changing significance. It is in your hands.